OUR OWN
LIFE STORY

Nicholas Corder

D0270626

Straightforward Guides
www.straightforwardco.co.uk

Straightforward Guides

© Nicholas Corder 2016

British-cataloguing-in-Publication-Data. A catalogue record for this book is available from the British Library.

ISBN
978-1-84716-649-4

Cover design by Bookworks Islington

Printed by 4edge www.4edge.co.uk

Also By Nicholas Corder

Non-Fiction

Escape from the Rat Race – Downshifting to a Richer Life

Learning to Teach Adults – An Introduction

Successful Non-fiction Writing

Foul Deeds and Suspicious Deaths in Staffordshire and the Potteries

Foul Deeds and Suspicious Deaths in Cumbria

Writing Good, Plain English

Creating Convincing Characters

Fiction

The Bone Mill

Plays

Nigel's Wrist

Jacobson's Organ

Cash and Carrie

Star Struck

A Midsummer Night's Travesty

Shagathon

Bingo Royale

Fire in Her Belly

Talent

Catching Lightning in a Bottle

Twilight Robbery

Acknowledgements

When you teach, you always learn more from your students than anyone else. So, this book is for all those students who have helped shaped the ideas that have gone into this book.

As ever, I'm indebted to my wife, Pauline, who keeps me going with cups of tea and coffee, reads early drafts and encourages me when the going gets tough.

I'd also like to thank Roger at Emerald Publications, who sticks with me as an author, despite the vagaries of the publishing world.

Lastly, but most importantly, I'd like to thank you for either buying this book or borrowing it from the library. You are a person of taste and refinement. I wish you the best of luck with your project.

Contents

Introduction

Summer 1919. A troop carrier pulls away from its temporary mooring in Newcastle-upon-Tyne. It is carrying soldiers under the command of General Ironside, destined for the White Sea port of Archangel. Here, they will fight in support of the White Russians, the Tsarist force that is attempting to wrest control of Russia from its new communist leaders.

Amongst the men on board, most of them already hardened by several years of fighting, is Sergeant Frederick Corder of the Royal Engineers, an exiled Londoner. He is essentially being paid a bounty for this trip, which he needs in order to have enough money to marry Ethel Pepper. Fred, a big, burly man, built like a rugby forward, is already a veteran of the Great War. He walks with a slight limp. He has been wounded in the knee and his left leg is now bent at an angle that gives him the nickname K-leg amongst his fellow NCOs.

In fact, shortly before my father's death I asked him where my grandfather Fred had been wounded.

'In the knee,' said my father.

'No whereabouts in France?'

'I don't know,' said my father. 'I never asked him about his war and he never asked me about mine.'

It was like this for men of those two generations, called up to fight in global conflicts. They talked little about these events. But this much I do know. Somewhere in Northern France or Belgium, Fred was shot through the knee and fell onto the barbed wire, providing a convenient human bridge for the others in his platoon to cross German lines.

Family lore also holds it that Fred's father was a violent alcoholic, who despite an excellent job in the House of Commons, drank his family into poverty. Fred himself is prone to sudden and irrational mood swings. He enlisted in 1913, as soon as he was old enough to run away from his troubled home. He certainly managed to establish a distance between himself and his family, whoever might have been at fault for this schism. When we came across him in the 1911 census, he had several brothers and sisters my father had never even heard of. Somewhere in here is a juicy tale of a huge family row whose details we will, alas, never know. Indeed, Fred never speaks about his childhood, save to lecture his own children on the dangers of alcohol.

So, there are scant details of Grandfather Fred's life. But among the tatty possessions that have been passed on to me is a photograph album that must have been started by him. It dates from an era when fewer photos were taken. Some of the pictures on the same page have intervals of 20 years between them. But amongst the handful that date from the 1910s are a couple of Fred, posing with fellow NCOs outside the Nissen Hut at a transit camp that also doubled as a convalescent camp. There are even a few pictures that date from the under-reported North Russian campaign.

Now, according to my late mother, by pure coincidence, amongst the crowds of well-wishers gathered on the quayside to cheer the ship on its way to the Baltic is a slim local lad called Roland Wood. Roland is one of six children living in the then fashionable West End of Newcastle-upon-Tyne. He is training to be an architect. He too has served in the Great War, but as a volunteer. He now wears a moustache to hide the scars left by shrapnel wounds, sustained whilst a young Second Lieutenant in Belgium, where he had been left for dead during a futile advance by the Northumberland Fusiliers. He has spent the last two years in and out of sanatoriums, fighting to regain the use of an arm that his father begged surgeons not to amputate.

Roland and Frederick were my grandfathers. They didn't meet on that day in 1919, but had to wait until 1951 when their youngest children, my parents, were married. Both of them died young by modern standards. I never knew Frederick and have only the faintest childhood memory of Roland.

The two men were ordinary lads, not untypical of their day and age. One was fortunate to live in relative affluence at a time when most city-dwellers lived in conditions that would horrify us today - their house was one of the first to have electricity in Newcastle. The other was unfortunate to have been reared by a desperate, alcoholic brute, but lucky enough to be intelligent, able and ambitious. They probably had no realization that they were living in extraordinary times. Both were lucky to have survived the greatest slaughter of young men in European history.

Readers of a certain age will surely remember the smoke-filled silences of the men who belonged to the generations who fought two wars. They rarely spoke about what had happened to them. One of my uncles used to relate a funny tale about meeting up with his two brothers on the beach at Dunkirk. This was the only story he ever told. Apparently, amongst the other things that happened to him was that he had to bury a baby on the beach. But all of this is just family stories, half-remembered, half-understood and, quite possibly entirely mythical.

If only we had more information about our own families. Wouldn't it be great if they had left behind something for us to read? How much better we might understand their lives and, thus, how the past has come to make us.

Like Fred and Roland, we all leave a few doodles of our own across the margins of history. In Fred and Roland's case, there are some stiff, formal photographs, usually in uniform, a few medals, a cigarette box. For years, my study wall boasted the clever, well-drawn copies of Mickey Mouse, Pluto and Goofy that Roland drew for my mother's bedroom wall in the 1930s, that had been passed around the family for generations of young children to enjoy and somehow, as is the way in families, found their way back to me. They are now in the keeping of my great-nephew Charlie. There's not much else.

Generations that follow us will find our names in the Census, on the deeds of properties, on electoral rolls, on membership lists in the archives of Trades Unions or professional bodies. We might have a box of keepsakes - the blazer badge, the school report condemning us as mediocre and lazy ('works well when pushed'), a love letter, a certificate of baptism, a commemorative coin...

Let me reiterate: not enough of us leave behind anything that will tell future generations what our lives were really like.

****

Section 1

Getting Started and Keeping Going

The past is a foreign country; they do things differently there. L.P. Hartley

In this section, we'll look at planning what you're going to write, from the gathering of materials that will help prompt memories through to deciding how to map out your book. We'll also begin thinking about writing a first draft of that all-important story - your life.

Chapter 1

Why Do You Want to Write Your Life Story?

Every one of us has a story to tell, so why not just get on with it?
I know there are some people who can just sit down at a desk and produce thousands of beautiful words that they will never have to change. They're the exception, not the rule. Most of us aren't like that. After all, if you felt entirely confident that you could write your life story without any help whatsoever, you wouldn't be reading this book.

So, to be blunt, why do you want to do it? After all, if you honestly intend writing something substantial, you are going to be taking up a good chunk of your life to do it. As well as taking up time, you'll probably also need industrial quantities of effort, coffee and chocolate digestive biscuits. Your reasons for writing your life story are probably linked to a second question: who do you expect will read your writing?

Writing for Fun

We human beings love to be creative. Writing your life story is an absorbing way of tapping into that side of your personality. It's also remarkably inexpensive. You only need pen, paper and a little time. Add into that some will-power and hot beverages and you're well on your way to keeping yourself amused over several weeks, although it's more likely to take months or possibly even years. As well as being a comparatively cheap hobby for which you've got most of the equipment anyway, it can also be pursued under almost any weather conditions.

If you want to get a more professional finish to your completed work, you may have to invest in a bit of computer kit if you don't already have it. But even then, writing is a cheaper pastime than cross-country skiing, paragliding or power-boat racing and your chances of injury lower.

Life stories written for the sheer fun of the project are often the best. You can tell when the writer has enjoyed the process of writing – it leaps off the page, involves you, makes you want to read on. Writing for the sheer enjoyment of recording your life is a great motive for doing it.

Writing for You and Your Family

If you're writing for the pure pleasure of writing, then your reader is likely to be just you or your family.

There's no reason why it can't be just you. Why not? What on earth is wrong in writing simply for yourself? There are plenty of people who are happy to dabble in watercolours without ever once wanting to display their efforts, even in the privacy of their own lavatory.

You can learn a great deal writing only for yourself. However, most of the life writers I have worked with want to write for their families. They want their children or grandchildren to have a record of their lives.

From my introduction, you can see that I wish I had more information about my two grandfathers, Roland and Frederick, and their lives. Just think how fascinating it would be for someone hundred years from now – perhaps one of your direct descendants - to come across a well-written document of your life. You might argue that Roland and Fred were involved in a World War and you've spent your life in the accounts department. Yes, it's true that not all lives are as colourful as each other, but that's not always for the best. Anne Frank led a far more intriguing life than I have, but she died in her teens. I'm happy to live a somewhat greyer life.

A moment's reflection and we can see that there are things we do now that will soon disappear into history. Emptying a cupboard the other day, I came across a couple of ash-trays. I haven't smoked for well over 15 years and just about everyone I know who did smoke no longer does. There was a time when non-smokers would even keep in a table-top cigarette-box to offer smokers when they visited rather than ushering them out into the garden to puff damply in the rain. A visit to a British cinema meant watching the film through a cataract of cigarette smoke. There were even little ash-trays screwed to the backs of seats. The current trend is towards 'vaping'. The electronic cigarette is taking over from the old analogue fag.

Recapturing a Lost Time

There are things that you do now that will eventually be as extinct as the dinosaur, so writing to recapture this is vitally important. And remember this: ordinary people are endlessly fascinating. Our lives may seem dull and trivial to us; but they are not. My grandfathers may well have believed theirs were too, but if they had only put down on paper some of their thoughts, if they had only taken a little time from their lives to write something about their experiences, we would know so much more. Likewise my grandmothers, who were also born before the age of the aeroplane.

The biographies of the great and the good, the noisy, the powerful, and the famous will always be recorded. The rest of us, the ordinary folk going about our ordinary daily lives are just as interesting - probably more so. Visit any stately home and you'll find that the kitchens are amongst the most popular parts of the house. People will move swiftly past the Vermeers and Landseers, but spend ages chatting to the curators about how the spit worked, where the scullery maid slept and what the butler's wages would be worth today.

It's a simple point, but one worth remembering - the way in which we go about our lives is constantly changing. My wife and I once lived in a Victorian terraced house, built for the station clerk of a minor branch railway. Even that family, hardly well-off even by the standards of the day, had a live-in servant, who would have performed the duties now carried out by your washing-machine, dish-washer, hand-held blender and the Tesco delivery van.

Technology advances and with it many of the old ways are lost. I'm still a good few years off my state pension, but as a youngster working in an office, I used a telex machine, a comptometer and a PABX telephone exchange. Slightly later on, as a young teacher, I created hand-written worksheets using a Banda machine, which at least gave the kids in my classes something to sniff before they nodded off. The year I took my Maths O-level (roughly the equivalent of GCSE if you're a youngster or School Cert. If you're an oldie), my teacher said that he reckoned that somebody would be bringing one of those new-fangled calculators before the school year was out. He was right. And that calculator had set some indulged lad's parents back about £30.

Jobs have disappeared. I once worked as a figure clerk. A small group of us had to take invoices and add up the numbers on them and pass them on to a crabby woman with terminal halitosis who then transferred our calculations into to a massive ledger that was wider than her desk. By this stage we had the fabulously modern technology that was a calculator with a built-in till roll that we had to share between six of us when crabby woman wasn't hogging it. Nowadays this kind of work is all done by a computer, which spits out automatic invoices, that are then mechanically folded into envelopes or increasingly sent via the miracle of the web to our home computers, where we open them and wonder how on earth they got the final total so badly wrong. We then spend a week trying to get a human being to sort it out. Indeed, just a generation ago, when such jobs as shorthand-typist and secretary were still commonplace, employment agents asked you if you knew how to use an electric typewriter. ('Can you work a golf-ball?')

Thirty years or so ago, it would have seemed an outlandish idea that I could type this into a computer, using a keyboard, then rearrange the text to suit me. A handful of people were just beginning to buy word-processors, often made by Amstrad. The daisy-wheel printer of my first word-processor, which you had to cajole into printing with a continuous sheet of folded, perforated, tractor-fed paper was so noisy, I had to put a towel underneath it to stop it from shaking the whole of my single-glazed, non-centrally-heated house.

The current generation manages to type into a telephone, which serves as calendar, notebook, camera, to-do list, giant reference encyclopaedia and just about everything else known unto humanity. And just with their thumbs.

They too, when they are old, slow and fat will wonder at how the generation that follows them simply attaches electrodes and 'thinks' their words into a gadget smaller than a cigarette packet. In a hundred years' time, someone will find this book in an antique shop selling such quaint items of yesteryear ('people used to read them you know') and laugh outrageously as the yellowing pages disintegrate under their fingers at just how wrong my predictions are before climbing into their driverless cars and swooshing off on autopilot to their sleeping pods.

What you do every day will fascinate the generations to come. And this is a great reason for writing your own story. And it doesn't have to be the whole of your life. It's also entirely valid just to write about a single episode or part of your life. You may simply want to tell the story of the years you spent in the army, or of your time as a Land Girl. Perhaps you were a nurse and want to show how things were in the old days. You remember the old Nightingale wards, the days when patients could smoke in the dayroom, when we had convalescent homes and the absolute fear of the hospital matron.

Maybe, you simply want to write about your travels. Just think how much this has all changed, even in the last twenty years. Once, even a trip from London to Paris was a huge adventure in exotica. Nowadays, the physical distance has been reduced by clever rail and aeroplane links. Where once we went to Morecambe, now we go to Mexico.

Amongst the odd things I've collected over the years is a small hard-backed home-bound book of collated, type-written sheets, picked up at a car boot sale (and will we one day have to explain what a car boot sale used to be?). It is bound in a dodgy green cover. There is a hand-written inscription in the front that reads 'To Jane and George – Memories of a happy holiday in France, August, 1950'. Now, August 1950 is still within the living memory of a good number of folks and a trip to France seems like a commonplace event. However, there is the fascination of a world that has already disappeared. As I write, Paris still exists, as does the Eiffel Tower, the Arc de Triomphe and the Champs-Elysées, all of which get a good mention. Other things, however, have altered dramatically.

We journey to France now by plane, roll-on-roll-off ferry, fast boat or the channel tunnel. No longer is it a fourteen-hours-or-more trip on the overnight boat-train lugging a wheel-less suitcase along the platform to the quayside or having your car winched in a huge net into the hold. The currency of France in the pages of this little home-bound book is the Franc (in fact, I suspect it may even be the old Franc), not the Euro. Nowadays, we can take as much money as we want in and out of France, but those were the days of strict currency control. I remember sneaking an extra £5 through in a shoe once, although I still wake in fear that I have been rumbled by the authorities.

And who in an era of electronic currency would spend an hour at a Bureau de Change waiting to cash travellers' cheques to pay a hotel bill, when you can swipe it onto your credit card in under a minute using contactless payment? Whilst we might all still see what the last of our holiday small change might buy us, we are not limited to half bottles of Benedictine and Cognac when we get back to British Customs. And who doesn't miss Duty Free? The author of this holiday journal also mentions the damage to the sea wall at Dieppe, but without any explanation as to why this should be of interest. Writing now, you would probably have to prod people about the Dieppe Raid, which was an assault on occupied France in August 1942 that went rather badly for all those involved.

The audience for this particular little car-boot find is probably just Jane and George, the traveling companions of Sybil and the anonymous 'I', its author. As such it is a testament to their friendship. It's an autobiographical gift.

It may well be that you simply want to write something similar. I think this is a great idea. This particular little green notebook is not of publishable quality. In fact, the author could have done with some of the tips in this book. However, it is based round one episode in someone's life. It is a record of their history and, as such, valid and valuable.

Reasons to Tread Carefully ...

All of us have been through events that trouble and disturb us. There are people we love who have died. We have broken marriages. We've done bad things to others, and been on the receiving end of a few raw deals ourselves. Some of us were traumatized by the most horrendous circumstances. Child abuse, for instance, was once swept under the carpet. There was a closed world of silence that cloaked it from the world. Now, at long last, some of the historic sins of people in positions of power, such as teachers, politicians, priests, public figures and parents have come to the surface and are being dealt with, if sometimes too late to bring perpetrators to justice.

You may have been through some horrendous events yourselves. Often, writing about these events can be very therapeutic. The very act of getting them out of our heads and onto a sheet of paper can make us feel a great deal better. It's the equivalent of the confessional box or the psychiatrist's couch.

I can't imagine there can be anyone who has gone through life without someone being unpleasant to them at some stage. Wouldn't writing an autobiography and exposing the charlatans, cheats, bullies and hypocrites be tremendous? Oh, to be able to stab in the front all those who have stabbed you in the back!

It could give you a great sense of release and renewed well-being. If published - even on the Internet or only as a few printed copies for family use - it could also get you into serious trouble (there's more detail in Chapter 12, which deals with pitfalls). More importantly, writing a book as a means of getting your own back is unlikely to make good reading. The chances are that you will come across to your reader as petty and resentful or even as downright nasty, no matter how much 'in the right' you are. You could have been the saintliest saint that ever petted a sweet, furry mammal, but you'll appear small-minded. Vindictiveness never looks good on paper. It makes the writer look worse than the original offender.

Yes, there has also been something of a fashion for what have been labelled 'Misery Memoirs'. This isn't a recent phenomenon, though. As far back as 1821, Thomas De Quincey published his account of addiction in *Confessions of an English Opium-Eater,* which included a section on the pains of opium. So 'misery memoirs' are not just a flash in the pan. There's nothing wrong in this. Writing out the demons is a great idea. However, you do need to think who will actually want to read what you've written. If part of your reason for writing your life story was to let other people share your experiences, simply having a good moan for page after page is not going to keep them glued to your words. You have to think how you can convey these terrible experiences to the reader without losing them. It's worth looking at writers such as Frank McCourt or Primo Levi to see how they deal with terrible circumstances in highly readable prose that pins you to the page.

The Wider Public?

It may be that you have greater ambitions for your work. If you do, more power to your elbow. There is nothing quite like the thrill of seeing your name in print. I once walked into a library that had twenty copies of a book of mine on the shelf and the thought of it gives me a buzz to this day. On the other hand, if I want to feel depressed, I can think of a couple of reviews that have left me feeling more than a little bruised.

I've already warned that getting a book published is hard work. Occasionally, there are memoirs or autobiographies written by unknown or obscure writers that become best-sellers. In the main, however, most publishers are not interested in autobiographies from unknowns. The chances are that our million-pound first -time author from a couple of paragraphs back is writing fiction (or dubious self-help) and has a TV series anyway.

You might write a classy little autobiography full of wit, warmth and wisdom that is turned down by every publishing house in the English-speaking world, only to find that the latest teen sensation from YouTube, personable and suitably vacuous, has been given a half-million pound advance for the story of her first (and only) twenty years. The book contains their entire wisdom and has a lovely, photoshopped acne-free portrait of the author on the cover. (Remember when photoshopping was airbrushing?)

It's not fair at all, but if you're old enough to be contemplating writing your life story, then you're probably old enough to accept the fact that life in general isn't fair.

I don't say this to put you off. If you've got a great story to tell and can tell it in a way that captures the reader's attention from the start, then you do stand a chance. I simply don't want to raise any false hopes.

No man but a blockhead

I've left the notion of trying to make money from your story till the end of this chapter. Most of the people I encounter who are writing their life stories are doing so to make a record of their lives for people who are close to them. If you want to cast your reading net wider, you enter a whole new arena.

Writing for money can sometimes look like a piece of cake. Money for old rope. Choose whichever cliché you prefer. It doesn't help that occasionally there's a big media story of the unknown author who secures a million pound advance for their book. There are three main reasons why we hear about this. The first is that because any book deal with these kinds of figures is highly unusual. The second is that the publishers want as much publicity as possible for their author so they can shift truckloads of copies to be able to pay for this ridiculous advance. The third is that the writer is an extraordinarily photogenic blonde in her late twenties with a penchant for wearing revealing clothing. What you don't hear so often is that publishers will often drop these authors after just one book if they don't sell the huge quantities they'd hoped to. The reality is that making money from writing is hard. It is also getting harder. Yes, some people make a good living, but plenty more - even well-known writers - are really making their income elsewhere, often by teaching.

I know Dr. Samuel Johnson is reported to have said 'No man but a blockhead ever wrote, except for money.' But I have to take issue with the old lexicographer. The chap turning out for his local pub football team is playing football. He may not be playing at the same standard as the players in the national team (although you may sometimes wonder), and he's certainly not making their kind of money. Importantly, he is not expecting to be paid for his efforts. Nor is he considered a blockhead just because he fancies a game of football without the prospect of a match fee, a win bonus and the extensive use of a Ferrari and a couple of nymphets.

There are plenty of things that can be done by professional and amateur alike. There is no reason why you have to make any money from your writing, unless of course you want to. However, as soon as you start trying to earn money from your writing, you are stepping into a different league. I know that's sometimes hard to believe when you read some of the shoddiest efforts that somehow manage to wriggle their way into print, but you are. There's no point getting morose about this. There are untalented people in all walks of life – or perhaps, more accurately, there are people whose talents would be better served in other jobs. Writing is no exception.

I will deal with selling your writing more fully in Chapter 13. For the moment, let me leave you with a thought. What may be extremely interesting to you, your family and your friends may be of no interest whatsoever to people who do not know you. And if you want to sell your writing, you are going to have to appeal to people who do not know you at all. After all, our pub footballer is, at best, expecting a couple of his mates and his girlfriend to come and cheer him on. He's not expecting a talent scout from Manchester United to come and sign him up whilst he's having his half-time cigarette. Writing is no different.

Appealing to the wider public may be hard, but you may find that your work does appeal to an audience beyond your family, but not to a nationwide one. Stories of local interest can often find a home in regional magazines, but would never be considered by national publications. You may not even get a fee. But if you can remember when the carpet warehouse that is about to be demolished used to be the local dance hall and have a good story to tell about when you used to shake a tail-feather there on Friday nights, then this is the kind of material a local or regional publication might be looking for.

This all sounds a bit off-putting, but some of my life-writing students have made it into genuine paid-for print. They had that ambition and aimed for it. So if that's your goal, then it is achievable - others have done it. I would like to think that this book can help you do that, but you do need to keep your feet on the ground. And even if you do achieve this goal, don't expect the financial rewards to be great. And, no, this isn't being pessimistic; it's being realistic.

Changing Ambitions

There's nothing wrong in deciding to write a few hundred words about the night your street was bombed during the Blitz and then deciding that you want to write about other aspects of your life as well. Nor is there anything wrong in trying to write an enormous 100,000 word biography and then deciding that really all you wanted to write about was the night your street was bombed.

For the sake of having some common ground, we are imagining that you are going to write a work of 50,000 words. That's roughly the length of this book. Of course, that's just pretend. In fact, it doesn't matter if you're writing a handful of episodes or an entire life story – the techniques and tips in this book will help you to do both. Nor is it wrong to set out hoping that your writing will find a larger audience only to discover that (sadly) nobody wants to publish you.

It's all a big adventure. You will remember things that you'd long confined to the dusty attic of your mind. You will discover things about yourself, your friends and family that you had never realised before....Enjoy the process.

****

Chapter 2

Stirring up Those Memories

In this chapter, I'm going to suggest some techniques you could use to help get your memories working well. Obviously, everyone has his or her own way of doing anything. I don't want to suggest that there is only one way of approaching your writing or, for that matter, for jogging your memory and any subsequent note-taking. So please feel free to use, adapt or even ignore what I say. Perhaps the best approach is probably to cherry-pick these ideas for the ones that suit your temperament and aptitudes.

Rough Notes (Can Be As Rough As You Like)

As you move through the processes we're going to look at, you'll want to take notes about incidents, people and places, otherwise all those fantastic thoughts and memories will drift away. Try to jot things down as they occur to you for the simple reason that you'll forget them if you don't. Don't worry at this stage about how neat your early notes are or what form they take. They are for your eyes, not for anyone else. The important thing at this stage is to be collecting material - the kernels of ideas, if you like - not worrying about how many marks your old English teacher would have given you for your handwriting.

One of the great things about writing is that nobody needs to see how messy the process is, because it's the end product that counts. I try to keep a small notebook in my pocket at all times and then transfer jotting to relevant larger notebooks as I'm often working on more than one project at any time. You might be more advanced and use a mobile phone or some other ingenious device, but the point is that as long as you've got paper and a few pens about your person, you should be able to jot memories and ideas down the moment they occur to you. A notebook is more efficient as this keeps all your jottings in the one place. Of course, you can just fire up the computer and start typing away. If that suits you, then great. But for many of us, getting some ideas together before we start writing means that what we end up writing is fuller, more interesting and ... well... better thought-out.

Thinking About Your Life

Despite their bad press, I'm a sucker for a Christmas Round Robin. During the Christmas break, I have a good catch-up on news. Yes, there are people whose letters are merely an exhausting list of how wonderful their offspring are, but I still like knowing what's going on. These letters are distilled versions of life. Each letter gives a bald précis of the author's year. We want to be aiming for something fuller and more interesting. It's too bland and banal to shorten a life into a couple of paragraphs. And the danger is that if you ask yourself a question such as, 'what have I done in the last 10/25/50 years?' what you say is still a boiled-down summary.

We sketch our lives in the briefest of outlines. Wrack our brains though we might, most of us will be able to point to only a handful of major life events. Somehow, we've only got the skeletons of our lives, but if we are going to write in any depth, we need the flesh for those rattling bones.

The biggest problem with trying to fill in some of the details is that the memory is a funny beast. It's always playing tricks on you. One moment you think you've grasped hold of some tenuous fragment of your earlier life and then it's gone. If you're anything like me, you can still quote large passages of poetry you were made to learn by heart at school, but can't remember the name of the person you've just been introduced to.

Even describing how the memory works is difficult. You can think of your memory as being a sort of Emmentaler cheese with more holes than cheese. Or maybe it's a bit more like an old muslin bag that you use for straining jam. Some memories squeeze through the little rips that have appeared over the years and are gone, but there are some bits that cling tenuously here and there to the gauze of the bag. Or perhaps it's a bit like having a rather ineffectual and temperamental shredder that you picked up at a dodgy table-top sale. Your memories are all written on sheets of paper and they are passed through it. Some pieces come out virtually intact, others are in large pieces, which can still be stuck together; others still are too fragmentary, or simply become paper dust and clog up the mechanism.

Whatever description you prefer – and if you don't like any of those descriptions, make one up for yourself, after all you're a writer – I'm sure you'll agree that even those of us with the clearest, strongest, most comprehensive memories need reminding about things from time to time.

You Can't Remember Everything

No-one can remember everything. Even if photographic memory exists (or eidetic memory if you want being strictly accurate over terminology), someone in possession of such faculties is never going to recall everything either. So, what chance a human being with a normal memory? And there's no point giving yourself a hard time for gaps in your memory - it's simply impossible for us to remember everything that has happened to us in our lives. Given that we can't remember everything, what we have to settle for is some strategies that might help us recover all that lost information. What we need are some tools for helping us to stretch our memories to bring to mind as much as we can.

Using Memorabilia

Some people are amongst nature's hoarders. They squirrel away every last memento of their lives, right down to bus tickets and notes to the milkman. Others are bleak minimalists, shedding every tiny scrap of everything remotely personal. Most of us hover somewhere on the continuum between these two extremes.

I'm not a great one for keeping much in the way of bits from my past. Every now and again, I have a good clear-out on the basis that parts of my house are being used for storage when they might be better used as living space. Nevertheless, I do still have my school reports (just to remind myself what an idle soul I am at heart), a couple of scrapbooks of the minor achievements of my life, a couple of photo albums and an archive of the articles, stories, books and plays I've written and had published (sad, I know, but it's my only claim to fame). For years, I also had the world's most impressive collection of rejection slips. But in the end, someone pointed out that this was mere self-flagellation, so they went to the great recycler. My old diaries, address books, postcards, letters and programmes from plays, football and cricket matches have also long been consigned to the recycling bin.

Even so, I've still got enough personal bric-à-brac to start putting together the story of my life. And if you are better at keeping personal records than I am, then you are in an even stronger position. Perhaps you are the kind of person who can maintain a diary religiously and keep all your birthday and Christmas cards. Perhaps you have drawers full of old correspondence. Perhaps you have scrapbooks and photo albums – maybe the photos even have captions. You can also now turn to whoever has to share your living space and declare, 'You know all the stuff you wanted me to chuck out, well ...' I'll allow you to decide on your own level of triumphalism (or nastiness).

For instance, many of us have the curled up photo of our senior school. The one where you had a pyramid of benches and had to stand or sit in height order. The camera taking this panoramic picture often had to pan across a vast distance. So, if you went to a large enough school and there was a particularly athletic kid in it, they could be photographed at one end, then the moment the camera's lens had passed on, jump down off the back, sprint along to the far end and re-join the ranks so as to appear on both ends of the photo.

Dig out an old an old school photo, and although you're unlikely to know everyone on it, you'll suddenly find the name of some long-forgotten classmate springs back into your mind.

Similarly, if you find an old school report, you'll be reminded of your teachers. Who were the tyrants who left you trembling in the corridor? Who were the gentle ones you were horrid to? Who were the inspiring ones who turned you on to a life-time's interest in their subject?

Whatever you have managed to stow away – it is a really good idea to gather your personal archive from around the house and spread it out over a table somewhere just to give you an idea of what you've got. Useful material you could gather would include:

- Diaries
- School reports
- Letters & postcards
- Photos
- Poems that someone in your family has written
- Old address books
- Programmes from plays, sports events
- Certificates, trophies or any prizes you have won
- Cuttings from the local newspaper
- The family tree

If you want to start backing up all this material, then there are some fabulous sourcebooks by Robert Opie with titles such as 'The 1950s Scrapbook' or 'The Wartime Scrapbook on the Home Front' in which you will find oodles of adverts, gadgets and other memorabilia from the relevant decade or era. These can be extremely useful. (See Appendix B for more information.)

Talking About the Past

Another good way of remembering your past is by simply talking about it. If you have brothers or sisters, I am sure you will be able to chat about childhood events. If you can, try to find people you haven't met in years – for instance old school friends or colleagues from years ago – and have a little reunion with them. You'll be amazed at how many memories are prompted by simply gossiping over a drink or two at a pub.

A few years ago, I was involved in a fascinating project involving people talking about their lives. As late as the 1970s, women were employed at the pit-heads of Cumbrian coal mines. Their job was to sort the coal from a conveyor belt, removing any rocks and impurities. The project had several strands, one of which involved collecting the oral histories of these women whose lives had been hard, tough and uncompromising. As they sat round the table talking of their past lives, almost everything that was said triggered an associated memory in another member of the group. Soon there was a bubbling hubbub of reminiscence taking place. Just a handful of two-hour sessions provided enough material for both a book recording their working lives and a play based on their experiences. Chatting is good.

However, the poor lady who had to transcribe all these reminiscences really had her work cut out. The pit-brow lasses in their enthusiasm to tell their stories did what we all did. They talked over one another, left sentences half-finished, weren't always audible. Whilst it was a nightmare to transcribe, it also produced memories that may not otherwise have been triggered.

You could always take the approach used by the oral historian Studs Terkel, who pioneered the recording of real life stories. As far as I can tell, he interviewed people on an individual basis. You might want this to sound a bit less formal and 'chat with' instead. You need to juggle the idea of being able to make a recording (or just notes) with the powerful cross-fertilisation that a group can bring.

Using Topic Headings

Another way to stir the memories is quite simply to jot down a few notes under a particular heading. Here are some that you might like to use. I've arranged them in alphabetical order, rather than trying to decide on any kind of order of importance. Obviously, some might not apply to you, and there may well be others that you would want to add. The huge advantage of thinking in terms of topics - or themes if you prefer - is that it enables you to follow up on ideas without the restraint of chronology.

Accidents and Disasters

Have you been involved in a major event? Was it anything like a national tragedy, such as the disaster at Aberfan or the shootings in Dunblane? Or do you see disasters as something smaller? The washing-machine breaking down just when you get back from a fortnight's camping trip? Have you ever been involved in an accident? Was it a car or a bike?

Ambitions

What did you want to be when you were a child? Did that change as you got older? Did you have ambitions other than job-related ones? Did you always want to climb a particular mountain, visit a certain country, meet someone you admired? Do you still have ambitions now? Are these ambitions for you or for your children and grandchildren?

Arguments

Do you remember any particularly unpleasant arguments? Who do you think came out on top? Have you had any that are so severe that they have broken friendships or family ties? Are there arguments you had that you lost and wish you'd won? Have you been involved in a row, stepped back and then been proven right (or wrong)? Are there any clever things that you wish you'd said at the time, but didn't occur to you until a week later?

Birth

Are you a parent? If so, what do you remember about the birth of your children? If you're a father, were you there for the birth? Have you had to act as an emergency midwife when someone in the cab you were driving went into labour? Do you remember the birth of siblings or other family members? How did their birth affect the pecking order?

Breaking the Law

Have you ever been in trouble with the law? To what extent? Did you ever steal sweets from the market? Or did you enjoy raiding the stationery cupboard at work? Have you ever fiddled your expenses or taken cash-in-hand for a job you did and then failed to declare it? Do you speed, tailgate or double-park?

Brothers & Sisters

Do you have any siblings? Are they older or younger than you? How did you get on with them as a child? How do you get on now? Are you closer to one sibling than the others? What do you remember about their interests and hobbies? The clothes they wore? Their boyfriends and girlfriends? If you are an only child, did you always want a brother or sister? What do your siblings do nowadays? Are they still alive?

Career

What did you aspire to do for a living? Did your parents hope that you'd be something else? Do you think you've had a career or a succession of jobs? What's the best job you've had? And the worst? Did you do a job that has since disappeared? Did you work for a large enterprise? Was there a works canteen?

Chance Happenings

Have you ever been in the right place at the right time? Did you find yourself forced to share a table in a café with someone famous? Have you ever had one of those bizarre coincidences no-one would believe if it was made up? How much of your life has been based on luck?

Children

Do you have children of your own? If so, who are they? What do they do for a living? How like you are they? Are you proud of what they've done? Have they gone on to have children of their own? Are there any other special children in your life? Have you fostered or adopted children?

Christmas, Easter, Eid, Passover, Hogmanay, Etc.

Are there any religious or national holidays that you especially celebrate? What do you normally do? Is there a set menu? Do you fast? Have there been any especially memorable occasions? What do you feel about events such as Christmas? Do religious holidays reflect your beliefs?

Death of Someone Who Was Close To You

How difficult was this for you? What were the consequences of the death? How long did it take you to recover? Were other people affected? What kind of a send-off did you give them?

Disappointments

Is your life filled with disappointment or are you fairly happy with your lot? What or who has disappointed you? Politicians? Friends? Family? Your career? The money you made?

Dreams

Do you remember any of your dreams? Are there any recurring ones? Are you a fanciful daydreamer? Do you conjure up images of other places - sand-fringed, blue-sea islands or ice-capped Alps? Do you sometimes dream that you made a different choice at some point in your life?

Everyday Disasters

What are the silly things that have happened to you? Did you drop your mobile phone down the loo? Did you lock yourself out of the house in just a nightie? Did your romantic dinner result in a minor house fire?

Famous people

Have you ever met anyone famous? What were they famous for? What were they like? Were you impressed or disappointed? How did they treat you? Were they friendly or stand-offish?

First Communion/Confirmation/Bar Mitzvah/Bat Mitzvah

Did you have one of these? If so, what do you remember about it? Did you have to dress up specially? Did you get any presents? Do you still hold with the relevant religion?

Houses

What do you remember about the various houses you lived in? Your childhood home? And the first place you lived in as an adult? Did you go through the stage of renting a grotty bedsit? Where's the best place you've lived? And the worst? What is the house or flat you live in now like?

Four Seasons – Spring, Summer, Autumn, Winter

Which is your favourite season? What do you like about it? What do you like or dislike about the others? Are there any particular activities that you always do in any season? Do you ski in winter and play tennis in the summer?

Friends

Do you have any lifelong friends? Who is your oldest friend? Which friends do you see most regularly? Why do you have the friends you have? Have you made friends through work or hobbies or through some sort of club? Or are you a bit of a loner? What do your friends think are your personal strengths and what are your weak spots?

Games, Sports and Hobbies

Are there any games you enjoy? Do you like board games, or do you think the 'board' should be spelled 'bored'? What do you do to while away any free time? Or are you too busy to have free time? Do you belong to a club of any description? A book group? A chess club? Do you play a sport now? Did you play at school? Did you play for a club? What level did you get to, or are you a complete duffer? How did you enjoy sport at school? Were you the star athlete or always picked last?

Grandparents

What do you remember about your grandparents? Were they kindly or overly strict? Did they let you get away with things that your parents wouldn't? Were they generous? What kinds of presents did they use to give you? Did they teach you anything? Did Granddad have a shed? Are there things you'd like to know about them, but can't find out?

Holidays

Do you remember childhood holidays? Did you enjoy beach trips or did your parents drag you round dusty museums? How do you choose to holiday now? Do you like chilling in the sun (as it were) or activity holidays? What's you ideal destination? Do you use a tent, caravan or campervan? What's the best (and worst) holiday you've ever had? Do you speak any foreign languages and use those when you go abroad?

Illnesses

What childhood illnesses did you have? Can you remember any other children who suffered from illnesses - polio, TB? Have you had any illnesses since? Have you had bits of your body removed? Do you have scars?

Marriage

If you have been married, what do you remember of your wedding day(s)? Who was your bridesmaid or best man? Did you have an expensive affair or manage to get by on a registry office, two witnesses and a pie and a pint in the local? Have you ever been a best man or bridesmaid/maid of honour? What's the most interesting wedding you've been to?

Money

Is money important to you? Have you ever made much money? Have you ever inherited any? Have you made any good investments over the years? Has that Premium Bond you were bought at birth ever won you anything? If you bought a house, how much did it cost? What has been your biggest money weakness? Do you wish you'd made more of it? Or is it of little importance to you?

Neighbours

What have your neighbours been like over the years? Have you ever had any difficult neighbours? If so, what did they do? Were they noisy? Did they keep old sofas in the front garden? Do you have tales of hedge wars or of kind neighbours bringing food when you were bed-ridden?

Obsessions

Do you have any? Have you ever been a superfan? With photos of your hero or heroine on your wall? Do you have to iron everything including socks? Do you follow a football team slavishly, no matter what division they're playing in? Do you have to dust every day? Do you collect anything? Postcards? Thimbles? Rejection letters?

Parents

What were your parents like - physically? As people? Were they strict or lax? Cruel? Kind? How did they meet? What jobs did they do? Did they have any particular ambitions for you? Did you get on with them? How do you picture them in your mind?

Pets

Did you have pets as a child? Was it a family pet or your own? Do you have pets now? How do you treat them? Are you strict or can they lie on the bed? If you don't have pets, why not? Do you and your partner have different views about them? Are you a dog person or a cat person?

Politics

Are you interested in politics? Do you belong to a political party? Which way do you vote? Why? Who do you rate as good politicians in your life-time? Have you ever had to contact your MP about anything?

Possessions

Are possessions important to you? Is your house cluttered or minimalist or somewhere between the two? Is there something you hanker after - a car, a designer handbag, a top-quality musical instrument? Do you have keepsakes? Do you have something that has been handed down the family?

Religion

Has religion played an important part in your life? Do you believe in a god of some sort? Did you sing in a church choir? Do you go regularly to church or the temple or the synagogue? Are you religiously tolerant? What do you make of faiths different to your own? Was anyone in your family devoutly religious or militantly atheist? Have you ever been to a religious ceremony in a faith other than your own?

Romance

Did you have crushes when you were at school? Do you remember your first love? Are you a romantic? Do you think Valentine's Day is important? Or is it just an opportunity for card shops and florists to make money? What's the most romantic thing you've ever done?

School, College, University

How did you get on at school? Did you enjoy it? What were your best subjects? Which teachers do you remember? What were the good ones like? And the bad? Did you ever have any run-ins? Do you remember any of their pet sayings? Their mannerisms? Did you do well? Did you go on to any higher levels of education? Teams? Clubs? Friends?

Shopping

Do you enjoy shopping? Do you see it as recreation? Could you spend a whole day at a shopping centre? Do you spend ages looking for clothes? Do you go to the supermarket or to the local shops? Have you got any local shops? Do you remember certain shops from your childhood? Are there any kinds of shops that you can't pass without going in and browsing?

Somewhere You Know Well

Is there a particular place you love? Why do you like it so much? Do you have to travel to get there? If so, how? Why is this place so special to you? Can you conjure up this place in your mind and write about it?

Strong Characters

Who are the people who've left an impression on you? Are they bullies? Eccentric? Are they great-grandmothers chained to railings to protest the closure of the library or successful business types? Is it someone who spends all their free time on charity work? What qualities do you admire?

Teenagers

What were you like as a teenager? Were you rebellious? Did you follow some kind of fashion - mod, rocker, goth, emo? How did you cope with your own children when they were in their teens? What do you think of teens today?

Tough Decisions

Have you ever had to make a hard decision? To leave work? To leave a marriage? To have a pet put down? To move somewhere you weren't sure about?

Triumphs and Successes

What do you think of as your greatest achievements? What has brought most pleasure to your life? What are the highlights on your CV?

War/Service in the Forces

Did you serve in the armed forces? Were you conscripted or did you volunteer? Did you enjoy your time? Did you see active service? Is there a family history of service?

Superlatives

Well, if you've jotted notes for all these, you may feel a bit exhausted, but let's look at another possible approach to jogging your memory. As well as thinking about various topics, another approach you might take is to think in terms of superlatives. Superlatives (best, worst, first, last, latest, friendliest, most exciting, etc.) is a useful idea at the planning stage as it forces you to think of the extremes of your life, rather than the more mundane aspects of it. You might consider writing about any or all of the following:

- My best teacher
- My favourite pet
- My first job
- My first love
- My most frightening experience
- My worst day
- My earliest memory
- My best holiday
- My favourite book
- My worst boss
- My first car
- My strangest dream
- My biggest nightmare
- My worst fear

I'll stop the list there. If you're going to use this technique, you will probably want to write your own headings. You can also end up with more topic titles than is strictly good for you. If you find that two topics overlap, think about how you might combine them. If one topic proves unwieldy, then think how to sub-divide it.

Over to You
An Old Photograph

Dig out a photograph that has important memories for you.

Until the advent of the digital camera - and perhaps especially phones with built-in cameras, people tended to take fewer photographs. You may, like me, be unlucky in having both a family who took few pictures and when they'd assembled them carefully into albums, then proceeded to throw them out. On the other hand, your father (and it nearly always is fathers in my experience) may have been a keen amateur photographer who blued most of his money on film and had his own darkroom. In which case, you may have a problem deciding which photo to use. For the sake of the exercise, just grab one, even if you do so at random. You'll see where I'm headed with this, anyway.

Get your notebook, paper, pen or pencil of your choice and quickly jot down some notes for each of the following questions. If you're not sure about any of them, simply move onto the next. Don't try to write in full sentences, just scribble away. You probably won't need more than five or ten minutes and it's not a bad idea to leave plenty of blank space in your notebook for all the things that occur to you after you've done the exercise.

Answer the following questions...(overleaf)

- When was the photograph taken?
- Where was the photograph taken?
- What do you know about this place?
- Do you know why it was taken?
- Who is in the picture?
- How come they are there?
- What is happening in the picture?
- What do you remember about the people in the picture? Jot down a few biographical details.

When you've done that, take a bit of a breather. Leave all your notes to one side for a day or two. When you come back to your notes, is there anything you can add?

If you want, you could start writing about the picture itself. After all, one way of structuring your life story might be to have pictures that you then explain to the reader.

Your Childhood Home

In your mind, go back to the house where you spent your childhood. Take each of the following places in turn and jot down a few notes about each of them.

- Cellar
- Attic
- Your bedroom
- Your parents' bedroom
- The sitting-room
- The kitchen

- The hallway
- The garden or the yard

Now take one of the rooms and describe it in detail.

Desert Island

If you are a listener to British radio, especially a Radio 4 fan, you'll probably know the radio programme 'Desert Island Discs'. If you don't, try searching for it on the internet. It's a simple half-hour radio show in which well-known figures are asked to choose a series of eight records (remember records?) that they would like with them should they be washed up on a desert island with only a wind-up gramophone for company.

Using a variation on this format and taking it a stage or two further, let's imagine that you are stranded on that famous desert island. Jot a few notes to answer each of the following adding a few notes of explanation as well.

- Which book would you take?
- Which piece of music would be your desert island choice?
- Which film? Would you be able to stand watching it over and over again?
- Which TV programme?
- Which frivolous luxury item of no practical value would you like to have wash up ashore?
- Who would you most like to have come and visit you?
- Who would you least like to have come and visit you?
- What would you miss most?

- And least?
- Would you try to grow anything whilst on the island?
- Is there anything you'd be frightened of on your own?
- How would you cope with the solitude?
- Would you like to be rescued? If so, how? By whom?

You might not feel the need to take it beyond note form and start writing in depth. You should at least get one or two useful kernels of ideas from this little exercise. Besides, if you ever do get well-enough know to be invited onto Desert Island Discs, you've already done your preparation.

****

Chapter 3

Planning Your Book

Once you've trawled your way through all the material you can muster, then comes the time to think about how you're going to write your story.

Now, you may not be much of a planner. There's nothing wrong in that. If you steam ahead and write your life story, that's marvellous. However, we bash-it-out writers often end up with a fair hotchpotch and then have to bring some order to our chaotic scribblings in order to give them shape.

If you're not a big planner or use a mixture of part-plan-part-write, bear in mind that you're going to have to put some structure in at a later stage and that there may be plenty of things that occur to you as you're busy tapping away on your keyboard that aren't precisely relevant to what you're writing. For instance, you could be writing about an incident at school when you were caught daydreaming out of the window, which puts you in mind of the time 30 years later when the poor window-cleaner fell off his ladder. You still need to note the window-cleaning incident down somewhere.

How Long Is It Going To Be?
Throughout this book, we are imagining that the project you are embarked on is a book of 50,000 words. This is only so that I, the

writer, and you, the reader, share some idea of the kind of task that's in store for you. The reality is that you have to decide how long your work is going to be.

If you are hoping that your finished manuscript will be published, it is more likely that your book will need to be longer than my suggestions. In fact, few publishers are likely to look at anything shorter than around 80,000 words and, indeed, 100,000 words is perhaps a more realistic target.

On the other hand, if you are writing for your own amusement and that of your family and close friends, then the manuscript can be any length you chose to make it. But the danger of trying to write 100,000 words is that you spin your tale out thinly and are left with too much padding.

If you are less experienced as a writer, then you might find that you are better off keeping your ambitions modest to begin with. You might like to concentrate on just one period in your life. Then, if you find that your words are starting to flow, you can expand your ambitions as you go along and write about other facets of your life.

If you start with the grand ambition of writing a full-blown book of 100,000 words and find that you only manage 30,000, it is easy to view this as failure, when it quite obviously isn't – you've written 30,000 words.

On the other hand, if you decide simply to write up a few episodes and then discover that you have produced 30,000 words, it can feel like a grand success. Of course, in reality, you've produced the same number of words whichever way you look at it, but doesn't the second approach taste more like victory than the first?

Bringing Order to Chaos

You should now be at the stage where you have started to collect a great deal of material and you should be itching to turn these memories into scintillating prose. You may be one of those people who simply likes to get straight down to the task of writing. Again, this is perfectly fine. Let me reiterate what I've just said - there are no rules for how you set about writing the story of your life.

However, some of us, if we sit down to write with no notes, nothing on a piece of paper to guide us, feel lost. We feel as though we've been set down on some Lake District Mountain without map, compass, guide (or even Kendal Mint Cake).

If you are one of that brave band who can simply sit down with a pad of paper, or flick on the computer and start working with no worries as to what you are going to write, then you will be the envy of most people reading this. If you don't feel confident about starting anything without at least some idea of where you're going, then some sort of pre-writing is essential.

Whatever structure you choose for your life story - and we'll look at this in more detail in a moment - you probably now need to get your material into some kind of shape. You want some system that will bring order to your notes. Large notebooks - normally A4 size are good for this, but they are a little bit inflexible, especially if you've decided on your topics, allowed a certain number of pages for each, then find that you've run out of space. You might find it easier to use loose-leaf paper and a file or folder, or even one of those concertina files, which means that you can slip in scraps and pictures and other bits and pieces into the relevant section. I have different notebooks for different projects and am currently a fan of the B5 size notebook, which is a half-way size between A5 and A4, but harder to find in the shops. Notebooks that fold flat with sewn bindings and flexible cloth covers, which reduce bulk and weight, get my vote. I tend to use notebooks in combination with a large pin-board, which normally ends up covered in pictures, post-it notes, bits of paper and snippets of ideas. The great thing about a pin-board is that it allows you to see an overall picture of where your work is heading.

Whilst you might be able to write an episode from your life, or even an entire chapter of a book at one sitting, you're not going to be able to do a whole book in one go. Using a pin-board is one way of giving you a visual guide as to how all those little separate episodes join up. You could equally well use the dining-table, but the drawback with that is that you have to clear everything away every time you want to sit down for a meal.

As with all these methods, the main point is that you need to develop a way that suits you. There is no single system of gathering and ordering your material. Do what works best for you.

Be Flexible

At almost any point in the note-making, note-organising, pre-writing, and the actual writing stage itself, memories will come back to you that you will want to incorporate into your work. Being flexible enough to allow this is important. Don't upbraid yourself because you'd forgotten something that turns out to be very important - this happens to everyone. Just accept the fact that this will happen (possibly quite often) and be flexible enough to deal with it.

Marinating

Another useful concept that you might like to consider is the idea of 'marinating'. In the same way as you might leave a piece of meat to soak in a sauce for some time, you can leave an idea or a fragment of a story to stew in the juices of the mind.

Rather than pushing on to finish the episode or to make as many notes about it as possible, leave it to one side. For generations, psychologists and psychiatrists and anyone who can hold a clipboard and looks good in a lab coat have been trying to work out how the human subconscious works. Don't worry yourself about how it works; just accept the fact that it does. In the same way that you come wide awake in the middle of the night with the words 'Alma Cogan' – the name you couldn't remember over dinner earlier that evening – so too will fragments of memory join up.

It's an incredibly strong technique to use, but don't expect it to work all the time. As with all things to do with the mind, your brain doesn't work with circuit board logic and you will still find that you haven't got a clue what the name of the woman who lived next door was called, no matter how long you leave it to marinate.

Dividing Your Work into Chapters (or Chunks)

There is no way in which you can write your book in one sitting. There is also no way in which a reader can read your book without it being divided into manageable chunks. Knowing how to divide your work is quite a skill.

One way of organising your book is arithmetical. If we have 50,000 words long, what's wrong with dividing the book into ten chapters, each of around 5,000 words? That keeps the maths simple.

Of course, it won't work as easily as that, but you might find that the idea that each chapter should be around the 5,000 word mark will help you to make the book feel balanced. On the other hand, there's also no reason why you should have ten chapters. Why not 14 or 17 or 20? There's also no earthly reason why chapters have to be of the same length. In the book you are holding, for instance, the shortest chapter is around half the length of the longest.

However, it's not always a simple question of arithmetic. You need to develop a feel for which bits fit with one another and there are as many approaches to this as there are autobiographies.

To begin with, you don't have to write about the whole of your life. You can choose just one part of it. This might be better described as a memoir rather than an autobiography. But if all you want to do is record the time you spent in the Merchant Navy, then just stick to that. Charles Bukowski's semi-novelised life stories include books on the years he spent working for the post office and his adventures when Hollywood came calling to make a film of one of his books. Memoirs have the distinct advantage of focussing on a certain period and mean that you're not necessarily having to think how to deal with all the 'boring bits'.

Nick Hornby's *Fever Pitch* is based round football matches, although it is much, much more than just a book about football.

Laurie Lee picks different topics for *Cider with Rosie*, with chapter headings such as *First Light, Village School, Grannies in the Wainscot* and *Public Death, Private Murder*.
Blake Morrison's *And When Did You Last See Your Father* concentrates on his father's life. It moves between memories of his

father when Morrison was a boy to the 'now' of his father's final illness and death.

For the sake of this book, I am going to suggest that there are three main ways of going about dividing your book – chronological, topics or themes, and episodic.

Chronological

If you are writing a chronological account, then you still need to divide your life up into chunks.

Your chapter headings might be something like:

- Early life
- School days
- National service – Malaya
- Working for the company
- Family life
- Big promotion and the big move
- Life in the boardroom
- Working for myself
- Retirement
- Where I am now

Theme or Topic Based

On the other hand, you might like to go for an approach that is more thematic - perhaps along the lines of the headings and questions used earlier in chapter - and which is based not just around the events of your life, but also around interests and enthusiasms. In this case, your chapter headings might be something like:

- Mother
- Education
- DIY
- Holidays
- Climbing the corporate ladder
- Our house
- Children and grandchildren
- My obsession with football
- Church

If you're worried about your readers not having information in chronological order, you can always include a timeline as an appendix.

Episodic

Similar to the theme-based approach, but what you're doing here is cherry-picking your best stories. David Sedaris does this in his humorous tales, such as those collected in *Me Talk Pretty One Day*. Here, he just picks little parts of his life and writes about them as a series of personal essays. And, whilst I am sure there is a reason for the order in which they appear collected in his book, it's not to adhere to the demands of chronology. It's a liberating method to use.

One of the best ways of finding out how you want your book to be divided up is to get hold of an autobiography that you have particularly enjoyed. Re-read it, noting down how the author divides the work, then try to use the same approach in your own work.

Over to You
Your Plan
We've just seen that there are essentially three ways to write your life story:

- Chronologically - start at the beginning and work towards 'now'
- Thematically/topically - choose a topic (e.g. our house) and write about that
- Episodically - tell little stories, maybe moving back and forth in time

Think about the advantages and disadvantages of each method. Which of these methods do you think would suit you best?

Charting Your Life
It's also extremely useful to build a chronology of your life. Whilst you may not want to write your life story in strict chronological fashion, it will certainly help you.

You could do this in a very basic way:

1960   Started school
1961   Tonsils removed
1962   Whooping cough

Or you might like to develop your chronology a bit further and make it into something of a chart, as in the example overleaf:

Year	Where I Lived	My friends/family	Events in my life	Holidays	School college work	World Events
1960	Brighton Albion Terrace ??What number??	Parents, sister Jean (8 this year) Mum must be pregnant with Tina New friend at school- Michael Wilson	Start school	?Holiday at home?	Bedlam Primary school- teacher- Mrs Clarke 'with an e'	Rome Olympics
1961	D.o	Tina born	Milk monitor Scotland- Aunt Lizzy's wedding Get T.V.	Scotland for wedding, plus visit York on the way	New teacher Mr Beetham very strict	Eichmann trial
1962	D.o	Michael Wilson leaves Brighton. New friends- John and Billy Soames	Aunt Lizzy's divorce- family scandal Dad builds a tree house- John Soames falls out. We get first car- Morris Traveller	Camping in Kent- V wet	Mr Beetham	World cup in Chile
1963						

Or you could simply put each year at the head of a page in your notebook and scribble in some notes.

Please don't be limited by my suggestions for headings. You can use whatever you see fit. You'd certainly want larger squares to write in all your notes, but you can see the kind of chart I'm suggesting. Many students on my life-writing courses like the general idea of a chronology such as this one and often adapt it for their own purposes. Some of the more computer-oriented ones have even created spreadsheets using these and other headings. Again, one of the many advantages of this kind of chart is that you can add to it whenever anything occurs to you.

So, if you think it would help you, why not do one for your life?

****

Chapter 4

Putting Pen to Paper, then Keeping Going

Climbing Mount Everest without a Sherpa

We've decided that your book will be 50,000 words. If it's the first time you've ever written anything that long, it looks like a daunting haul. 50,000 words! How on earth am I ever going to do it? It's like climbing Mount Everest without a Sherpa or oxygen.

It's at this stage that you may start looking round for some excuses to avoid writing. These may range from the highly practical, 'I must clean the cooker' to the pseudo-arty, 'I don't feel as though the muse is upon me today'.

You can prepare to write for ever. You can shuffle your notes, photographs, chronologies and diaries, moving them like armies around your desk. You can read everything you've written for the 63rd time as well as a pile of other people's autobiographies, but if you are going to write your life story, then one day, you have to sit down and start.

It's that obvious, really.

If it's any consolation to you, every writer I know has huge tussles with themselves and their consciences before they get down to any serious work. One friend of mine says that you can always tell when he has to write something, because you'll find him cleaning the house. He's not the world's most house-proud man either, so when cleaning beats writing, you know that writing must be hard work.

Well, it is ... and it isn't. Writing is not as tough of the genuine toil of a North Sea trawlerman, coal miner, social worker in a tough neighbourhood, police officer, a soldier in battle or the parent of children going through puberty. All these jobs are a lot harder than sitting at the computer keyboard and flailing away with a couple of fingers for an hour or so. Most writers would agree that the toughest part of being a writer is the self-discipline – the sitting down and keeping going. It can also be tough when you've been wrestling with the same material for ages and feel bored with it.

If I can write a book (and I've managed a fistful of books, plays and novels so far), so can you. My school reports (yes, kept in that famous box in the loft) are littered with such phrases as 'lacks self-discipline', 'works well, but only when pushed' or 'he has shown no effort whatsoever this year'. I have to chain myself to my desk and suffer caffeine poisoning to get anything done at all.

So, don't be put off as you gaze towards that 50,000 word summit. There are several techniques, tricks and ideas that you can use. Think of them as your own little writing Sherpas or oxygen cylinders.

Break the Job Down Into Smaller Chunks

When you start with a blank page or computer screen, the task looks formidable. You'll probably want to snap this book shut and slope off to watch Coronation Street or Eastenders.

If you're anything like me, you'll have a soft spot for a chocolate biscuit. You probably couldn't eat a wholesale size box of them at a single sitting, but if you managed a couple each day, eventually you'd have eaten the whole box. Instead of thinking of your book as one big job, break it down into smaller ones. This book is divided into chapters. The chapters are then sub-divided into topics and themes. Break it down into parts and it makes the job easier and a lot less daunting.

If you're going to write these 50,000 words and decide you can write about 500 words a day, then in 100 days - a little over three months - you will have a rough draft. If you can manage 1,000 words a day, then you'll have a complete rough draft in around seven to eight weeks. Doesn't that sound encouraging?

Sure, it will need revising and checking and there'll be bits you hate and have to change, but at least you will have something to work with.

If you find it a bit of a slog, then for each chunk of writing you do, promise yourself a small bribe. Award yourself a cup of coffee when you get to the end of the page. Yes, you could wander off and get one at any stage, but until you reach the bottom of that page, you're not going to have one. Another trick is to set a kitchen timer for 10 minutes and tell yourself you'll just write for that amount of time. With luck, when the buzzer goes off, you'll be immersed in your task.

Get the Writing Habit

After we leave school, most of our writing tends to be work-related, if we write at all. Our English becomes mangled by the demands of reports, specification documents and email. Management speak is probably the worst offender here. It obfuscates meaning in an attempt to be clever and is riven with clichés and unnecessary formalizations.

On the rare occasions when we do write something a little more creative, we probably do so in a flash of inspiration when a great idea occurs to us. Many of us can manage a funny poem for Barry-in-finance's leaving do or a few lines about our holidays in the Christmas round robin, but professional writers write every day. They get into the habit of making sure they are inspired the moment their bottom hits the seat. They can't afford to wait until the muse condescends to pay them a fleeting visit. This can be quite demanding.

So, get the writing habit. It's like anything: the more you practise, the easier it becomes. It will also seem less like a chore if you manage to make a short burst of writing part of your daily routine.

Finding the Time to Write

Given the fact that we have machines to do our washing, washing-up, clean our carpets, take us to work and perform so many other tasks that would have taken our forebears days to do, why is it we always seem to be squeezed for time in the modern world?

When people retire, they're constantly amazed at how much time their various activities take up. A common cry is 'I don't know how I found the time to work'. If they found the time to work, they can certainly find the time to do some writing.

Yes, but there are family commitments, free nursery care for the grandchildren, work pressures and you want time simply to relax. Agreed, but if you look at your weekly schedule, I am sure that you can find some slack. You don't have to set aside hours at a time - in fact you might find that in three slots of 15 minutes, you get just as much work done as you do in one of an hour. And those three lots of 15 minutes are easier to find than a whole hour.

If you can set aside longer periods to do some writing, then do so. I use the morning for writing and also try to get an extra hour's uninterrupted writing at some point in the late afternoon or early evening. During my writing periods, I break off every 30-40 minutes, have a coffee, check my email, make a few notes and so on. I try to relegate all the other bits of my work to later in the day. It doesn't always work out that way, but at least that's the intention. Yes, I know I write more-or-less full-time, but there was a stage when I had a proper job and slotted it in. Note that I don't exactly flog myself to death - my attention span is poor. I know this and get round it by breaking the day into smaller chunks. However, once in the groove, I don't tend to notice the time passing. And you can easily outdo me here - you can't be as idle as I am; it's not humanly possible.

If you need to 'make' time, then there are ways it can be done. Television eats into our lives enormously. We often just switch it on for a bit of background noise. One way to stop it encroaching on your writing time is to record the programmes you want to watch and view them later. If you record TV shows broadcast on commercial channels, you can cut out all the adverts - often as much as 30 minutes of a two-hour programme. You'll also be surprised how many TV shows you 'just had to watch' languish for months, unviewed, when recorded onto the hard disk recorder.

Clean the house a little less often, mow the lawn when it needs it, not just because it's Sunday. Make the kids or your spouse do more than they normally do.

Get up half-an-hour early before the rest of the household is awake and write during that time. Force everyone out of the house one afternoon a week and use that time to write. If you're still struggling to find time, then get yourself a book on time management or, if you prefer, simply record everything you do in the course of a week and look for little gaps you could use. Remember, your writing 'slot' does not have to be a huge amount of time. Write 100 words in ten minutes and you are making progress. Write nothing in two hours, and you're not. How long does it take to boil potatoes? A sentence? Two paragraphs? A side of A4?

When you're writing, one nifty trick is to remove your wrist watch. If you've got a little clock on the corner of your computer screen, cover it up. If you've got one on the wall or shelf, turn it round. Many of us have the bad habit of looking at our watches all the time. I'm convinced that looking at your watch when writing actually physically slows down the earth's rotation, so everything takes longer.

Writing Space

If you have a room you can set aside for writing, then that is ideal. If you're not fortunate enough to have such a place, then you're probably going to have to make do with a corner of a bedroom or even the kitchen.

If you are a wandering soul, you might like to write in different places around the house. Some people adore writing longhand in cafés with the hubbub of strangers around them. One of my friends goes and sits in the caravan in her garden for peace and quiet. Another of my students recently bought a garden shed, just to write in. I'm a shed writer. Mine is a summer house that has been dry-lined and insulated and has heat and light. It's probably a bit posher than you might want to go, but came in at a lot less money than one of those ultra-smart garden studios they advertise in the back of the Sunday supplements. I have an elderly second-hand laptop I carry out there, but do all my printing indoors, so don't have to worry about my paper getting damp. Out in Writing Shedquarters, the internet is a bit dodgy, which I know I could remedy with a relay system of some sort, but it keeps me off email and Facebook. If there's anything I want to research on the net, I make a note and look it up later. So, the shed also keeps me on the straight and narrow.

Many of us like a fairly fixed place to work. It's good to be able to spread your work out on a table or a desk and not to have to worry too much about how tidy it looks. Whatever you opt for, make sure you use that space as often as you can.

The Mechanics of Writing

Some people swear blind that unless they use an antique fountain pen, handmade paper and purple ink squeezed from the shells of the female Akhbar beetle, found only in the deepest jungle of Sarawak, they cannot wring out a single word. Others use an old ball-point and the backs of envelopes. Some writers swear by their ancient portable typewriters; some work directly onto a word-processor or computer.

Frankly, it doesn't much matter which method you adopt. I type directly onto a computer. Never having learned to type properly, I find it easier than copy-typing handwritten work. Occasionally I use an elderly piece of apparatus - an Alphasmart Dana word-processor - which has a tiny screen, but a very comfortable keyboard and can be linked to my computer. So, it's fine for bashing stuff out, has an astonishing battery life, weighs very little and can be used on trains or in cafés. Yes, there are all sorts of technologies that have overtaken it - but they all tend to take you towards the Internet and some require you to be online to use them, so tempt you into web-surfing, email or even games, rather than actual writing. Never forget that the Internet is a twisted vortex that will suck you into its world and only let you go when you've wasted at least half a day.

You might also find it useful to look at a piece of software called Scrivener. It's a word-processing app (or a text-processor if you prefer) that allows you to have several documents within the same-over-arching file open at the same time and to see what they are. You can easily move those documents around within the same file, which makes re-ordering a doddle. It also enables you to plan work easily with a built-in computerized corkboard. I've used it for everything from articles to a doctoral thesis. It's also compatible with most other word-processing apps, so once you've done all your basic writing and structuring, you can compile your work as a document file and then work further on it in the word-processing app of your choice. You can have a 30-day free trial of Scrivener and there are plenty of instructional videos on the web to help you.

Do Not Disturb

Ring-fence your writing time and space. If you plan to write on Thursday evening from 8.00 till 10.00, then put it in your diary, exactly as you would an appointment. If anyone wants you to do something on Thursday evening, you have to turn them down, no matter what. You are only allowed to break this rule if it's

Rosamund Pike on her knees in a negligée waving World Cup Final tickets or George Clooney with tickets for Wimbledon Centre Court or some equivalent.

Don't answer the phone. If you can't appoint anyone to answer it on your behalf, invest in an answer phone. I know they cost money and you may end up returning a phone call to another hemisphere, but at least you'll be writing.

Banish all members of the family from wherever it is you have chosen as your writing space. If you make your writing time fairly short and to a regular pattern, then it is easier not to have it disturbed. Stress to them how important a project this is for you.

Buy one of those signs for the front door that warn anyone trying to sell you anything that you keep Pit Bulls, Rottweilers, a pride of free-range lions and a Taser. If a campaigning politician comes to the door asking if they can count on your vote, tell them they can. This rule holds no matter what your politics, their politics or the overwhelming desire you have to let loose the Pit Bulls, Rottweilers and lions or have a real go at them with the aforementioned Taser. It's a well-known fact that if you say you'll vote for them, they go away. If you say you won't, they stop to argue.

Editing Brain versus Writing Brain

Many writers have commented about there being two halves of the writer's personality. First, there is the free-flowing part that allows you to crack on with writing. Then there is the editorial, censoring, checking part that nags constantly and says things like:

- You don't spell it like that!

- You can't put that!
- You've already said that!
- You've used that word three times in the same sentence!
- Somebody's written that kind of thing before!
- Call yourself a writer? I've seen more interesting telephone directories!

Editing Brain uses far too many exclamation marks as it is always positively outraged. Often, we find that we block ourselves from writing, simply because Editing Brain takes control and pooh-poohs everything we're trying to do. I think this is especially true of anyone who had the kind of Victorian education that managed to thrive well into the second half of the 20th Century, when accuracy and grammar were king and thought and creativity often had to take a back seat.

Of course, at some point you need to read your work with an analytical eye, but the trouble with criticising what you are writing too early on is that your writing isn't ready for it. It's not a bad idea to never show anyone your first draft. More often than not, first drafts are always messy, full of broken sentences, poor grammar, questionable spelling, and half-formed ideas. Mine look like the crazed scribblings of an orang-utan on acid. Editorial Brain is a useful chap to have, but you don't want him interfering whilst you're just trying to write. You want to use the free-flowing Writing Brain and you don't need outside criticism yet.

Writing Brain simply forges ahead, getting all the work down on paper. Editing Brain can only carp and correct. He's a bit like a critic and, as Brendan Behan said, 'Critics are like eunuchs in a harem: they know how it's done, they've seen it done every day, but they're unable to do it themselves'.

Keep Editing Brain out of the way at the moment. I'll show you how to use him effectively in Section 3.

Don't even stop to check dates, spellings or precise facts unless they make a real difference to your story. It's just too easy to get side-tracked, especially if you're hooked up to the dreaded Interweb of Disappearing Hours.

Is it spelled 'Springbock' or 'Springbok'? Oh, now that's interesting, there's something called Spring Canker Worm - they're a kind of caterpillar and they can destroy an entire orchard, I hope I haven't got them - oh, no it's just in parts of the United States. So what's this Spring Vetch, then? It's a kind of weed or tare. Weren't tares in the parable of the sower? Let's have a look, then. No, it doesn't seem to be that one. Where did I put the family bible? Now, weeds and tares, that rings a bell. Can't find it. My mother might know. Yes, hello, Mum. Yes I know I phoned yesterday, but ...Oh, she's not is she? So how did that happen? No, I'll ring her straight away.....

Before you know it, your writing session has ended up as something else altogether. If you need to find something out later, either jot it on a piece of paper, highlight it in your handwritten text or, if you're typing onto a computer, type in a line of 'xx'. When you come to check your work, simply click on 'Find' and enter 'xx' and then you can work at putting in the correct spelling, information, date, internet reference or whatever.

Don't be frightened to go where your mind takes you if it's at least relevant to your writing. If you suddenly find yourself flipping from one idea to another, just write them down, or at least jot down a couple of notes for writing up later. As I write this, I have my notepad open on my desk and am working intermittently on three chapters at the same time (which is easy in Scrivener software). I'm allowing my Writing Brain to do the work. I can tidy it all up later.

Keep a Progress Chart

Do a progress chart. I do two for each book. It's a childish ploy to give me a sense of achievement. One of them is a simple word-count. I keep track in my Scrivener software, which tells me I've actually passed my target of a thousand words for this session, which sounds very encouraging, but then tells me how much more I've still got to write, which swiftly brings me back to earth. I used to use a wall-chart and colour in the squares, but you've got to move with the times. The other word-count is on a spreadsheet and is a chapter-by-chapter word count, that way I can judge if any of them are either too long or too short and it's easy to see which need additional ideas, ruthless pruning or possibly splitting or amalgamating.

Music

If you find it useful to have music playing in the background, then do so. Stephen King goes in for heavy metal music. Some writers find modern songs distracting. Baroque music or Gregorian chant are my personal favourites. Indeed, it may be the case that if you can find music that plays at around 60 beats per minute you could be on to a winner. Some people suggest that as this is roughly the speed of a beating heart, this produces an alpha state (whatever that might be) and is thus good for thinking. I don't really listen to them, it's just that they cover those unwholesome silences when the keyboard isn't clattering. I can't manage to listen to spoken word radio (far too distracting) or to any of my favourite songs as I'd only want to sing along with them or check the lyrics out on the web.

Don't Expect What You Write to Be a Work of Genius

Let's be blunt. If you were going to win the Nobel Prize for Literature, you'd probably be well on your way now. You wouldn't be reading this book. I'm not going to win it either - which is why you get to read this.

J.B. Priestley said, 'write as often as possible, not with the idea at once of getting into print, but as if you were learning an instrument.' You can't expect to pick up a violin one week and be soloing with the London Philharmonic the next. Writing is a skill that needs some practice. There is no reason why, with a little exercise, you can't produce good, polished writing. You're unlikely to produce it at your first attempt, though, which is another reason for bashing it out and worrying later.

Make Some Writing Friends

Writing is a solitary activity. In extreme cases it can lead to real isolation. If you are at all sociable by nature, try to make sure that you also do plenty of socialising in between writing sessions.

You may find it worth your while to mix with other writers. You could join a writers' group or enrol on a local adult education course should such a thing still exist. Alternatively, you might find that a few days spent away on a residential course could give your writing a boost. If you're of the right age, then your local University of the Third Age might run a writers' self-help group.

Find a writing partner. By that I don't mean someone who will co-write your book, but someone who is on a similar wavelength to you. Many people find it useful, exhilarating and encouraging to get together from time to time over a cup of coffee to discuss progress, each other's work and to escape from the loneliness of writing. But don't use it as an excuse not to do any real writing.

Read, Read, Read

Read as much as you can. There are some wonderful autobiographies and memoirs out there. Browse your local bookshop and library shelves. Get out as many as you can and read them. Work out just what it is about a book that you like or dislike. There is a list of books that I've enjoyed over the years in Appendix A. You will doubtless have favourites of your own. Remember that bad writing is worth reading as much as good writing. It shows us useful mistakes and it also makes us say 'Hang on a minute. I could do better than that.' It becomes a challenge.

Writer's Block

Some people reckon that this doesn't exist. I'm not sure. It's hard to write if you've suffered some kind of personal tragedy, but I suspect that most writer's block is just a variation in output. I'm not quite sure why writers are particularly affected by this. After all carpenters don't get wood block, drivers don't get road block and sewage workers don't get toilet block. Perhaps it means that you can put your hand to your fevered brow and go, 'But, darling, I'm an artist!'

Maybe that's too flippant. Ask any writer and they will tell you that there are some days when every word feels like they're passing a gallstone, and yet there are other days when time flies by and, instead of the 500 words they had promised to write, they've managed half a book. Most writers I know can go from the kind of miserable day when squeezing words out feels like a self-imposed torture of the cruellest kind to other days when their fingers fly and the words come easily. Accept the fact that you're unlikely to write the same amount at each writing session.

On the days when the words don't flow, it can be a most upsetting experience. You can feel wretched and useless and miserable, despite the fact that all you're doing is writing - or not managing to write, more precisely. You haven't failed to put out a forest fire or to save a baby's life or to talk the aliens out of destroying planet earth, but your little world can seem insurmountably bleak. So, here are some tricks you can use to get yourself writing.

First, write anything - a shopping list, a postcard to Auntie Flo, a letter to an old school friend, a note to the milkman if you still have one and, if you haven't, a quick hundred words about what it used to be like when you had one. Imagine that you are a world-famous writer and that these little scraps of your genius will one day be auctioned for unheard-of sums.

If you're still stuck, try looking out of the window. I can see my wife doing some sweeping up along the back path. One of our bushes has come into bloom and the flowers are a frothy purple. The daffodils are somehow still perky, but look as though they have only a few days left in them. The grass in our lawn is beginning to muscle up besides the moss and weeds. It needs a cut. The patio needs pressure-washing and an old rotten bench needs taking to the tip.

What can you see from yours? Note the colours, the shapes, any people or animals or movement you can see. Start writing down anything you can.

Do something different. If you've got a dog, walk it. Take a letter down to the post office, go for a ride on a bus or a train. Drive to a place you like. Go to a café with your notebook and jot down anything about the people around you.

Get hold of a truly badly-written book and cheer yourself up in the confident knowledge that you can write better than that.

Leave a sentence half-finished, so that next time you come to write you are at least part-way through your first sentence of the day.

Do something else that is connected with your writing. For instance, you could try to make a list of everyone who was in the netball team at school, what toys you owned as a child, the weddings you have been to, who worked with you in your first job, all your teachers in Primary School.

Alternatively, pick out a few old photographs and try to remember where they were taken or if each has a little story.

Look through your old address books to see if any of the old names stir up memories.

Instead of thinking of it as 'writing time lost', try to think of it as some other kind of time gained. File some paperwork, clean the kitchen floor, de-worm the cat. Do any of the little jobs that you've been waiting to do. No, you won't get any writing done, but at least your house won't be as messy.

Make sure that your writer's block isn't simply caused by setting yourself unrealistic targets. Have a look at the number of words you are expecting to write in a session and revise them if you think you're being over-ambitious.

If you're really still stuck - give up for a few days. There is no point in forcing the issue. If the words genuinely won't flow, then you're only depressing yourself by not achieving anything. Leave it for a while. Your writing ability will return.

Don't Worry if It's Been Done Before

Evelyn, who joined a weekly class of mine several weeks after it had started, was hoping to write about her life as a district nurse. When she discovered that another student, Rita, was also writing about her experiences as a nurse, she was worried that she wouldn't be able to do it. After all, wouldn't she just be writing exactly the same thing?

As it happens, although they did similar work, Rita's story is set in the harsh, poverty-stricken streets of early 1960s South London. Evelyn's idea was for a rural tale of Cumbrian farmers, with life at a slower pace. Although both Evelyn and Rita write well and with warmth, humour and perception about the people they meet, they are two different people, so their stories come out very differently.

Remember - everything anybody writes has been written before. There are no new stories, but there are variations on a theme. The fact that YOU are writing it is what makes it different.

Once you've run out of excuses as to why you can't write, the time has come to get on with the writing.

How Do the Real Writers Do It?

New writers often feel that there can only be one way to write a book. They want to know exactly how a writer gets down to the task in hand. Once they have the secret of how to sit down and write, then the words will flow.

The public perception of writers is that they swan out of bed well after sunrise, mix themselves a Campari-soda to take away the taste of last night's champagne, perhaps do a spot of marlin fishing off the Florida Keys, then it's back home to knock out a few pages of witty and perceptive dialogue on a balcony overlooking the infinity pool, before a dinner-suited first night of their West End play. Otherwise it's six-hour lunches with agents and publishers, whilst their personal stockbrokers relay them hot-tips for the Next Big Thing.

Of course, there's nothing like a fantasy to get in the way of reality. In the main, writers just get on with the job, using whatever method suits them best.

Stephen King writes in the mornings, leaving his afternoons free for business matters and sleep and the evenings free for his family.

The late Barbara Cartland would drape herself along one of her pink sofas and dictate her books at the speed of sound to at least one of her four secretaries.

Joseph Heller, author of the great 'Catch 22', wrote his masterpiece by getting up early in the morning before commuting to his job as an advertising copywriter.

Roald Dahl, one of the most popular children's authors of all time, who had certainly made a great deal of money and could easily have afforded the poshest of offices, continued to work in his garden shed with a wooden board on his blanket-swathed knees, writing long-hand in pencil.

James Herriot wrote in the evenings, after work, in the middle of his family with the television blaring and he didn't fare badly with his autobiographical books at all.

For some, it's the stationery. John Steinbeck swore by Blackwing pencils. Bruce Chatwin adored his Moleskine notebooks.

Jack Kerouac wrote 'On the Road' on an old typewriter, using a continuous roll of paper, so that he didn't have to waste time re-loading individual sheets. Apparently he wrote it in two weeks - but that's Benzedrine for you.

There are as many ways of writing as there are writers. There is no 'right' way to set about your task. Avoid those writers who insist that there is only one way to go about it. Yes, it's handy to know what other writers do. You might find that they use some method that you could try out and, if it works, use it from then on. It's also always cheering when you find out someone famous uses the same techniques as you - you must be doing it right. However, the fact that Virginia Woolf, Roald Dahl, Philip Pullman and George Bernard Shaw are all shed-writers may make me feel good, but it doesn't elevate me into their company.

Simply find out what works for you and do it. The more often you do it, the easier it will become. However, one caveat: if you have to have things 'just right' before you can settle down to the task, then you might be creating a problem for yourself. The more rituals and demands you have, the harder it becomes.

****

Section 2

Writing Techniques

We never do anything well till we cease to think about the manner of doing it. William Hazlitt

When we write, we have a duty not to bore our readers. Bore them and we'll soon lose them. If you're going to put in all this effort, you want someone to read the results, don't you?

A great way of making your writing stronger and more colourful is to think like a fiction writer, rather than an autobiographer. There is no reason why you can't use many of the techniques that novelists use to hook their readers and make their books exciting.

The following section looks at some of those techniques and gives a few examples. You might like to try them out for yourself. If you do, you will soon find that they become an automatic part of your writing, making your story livelier and more interesting.

Chapter 5

From Narrative Summary to Writing in Scenes

Narrative Summary

As its name suggests narrative summary tells the story, but in brief terms. It can be really useful when we want to move quickly from one time to another:

> *After 3 years, I was moved off the shop floor and given a scruffy little office just behind the print machine.*

Or

> *We lived in that house for fifteen years, but when retirement came we fancied a move to the seaside.*

Narrative summary gets us over a bit of a dull patch and moves the action forward. However, it begins to get a bit leaden if it is the only approach the writer takes. Imagine reading pages of material such as this:

> *My family has always worked the land. For generations, we have been farmers and woodsmen. My great-great grandfather's first job was at about the age of six or seven, when he was paid to scare crows off the crops. My great grandfather bought the farm. In those*

81

days, it came with perhaps twenty acres. It was my grandfather who saw the opportunity to expand and bought various fields and even a couple of other small farms, so that by the time my father inherited, he had over a hundred acres. He was lucky that he was an only child as otherwise, the farm would have had to be divided as it was when it came our turn to own it.

It's hard not to think of your own life as a series of pieces of information. After all, the likelihood is that the nearest you've come to writing a life story before is in the pages of a CV, and these are often a fairly lumpen précis of work-related achievements. It's perfectly natural to use this kind of writing, but the above example is laden with dull facts that the reader has to chew their way through before getting to anything interesting. When you use narrative summary, try to make it as interesting as you can. Here's a little extract from Laurie Lee's *Cider with Rosie*, which shows how you can inject life into a summary and create something a little more exciting:

My Mother was born near Gloucester, in the village of Quedgeley, sometime in the early 1880s. On her own mother's side she was descended from a long static line of Cotswold farmers who had been deprived of their lands through a monotony of disasters in which drink, simplicity, gambling and robbery played more or less equal parts. Through her father, John Light, the Berkeley coachman, she had some mysterious connexion with the Castle, something vague and intimate, half-forgotten, who knows what? But implying a blood-link somewhere. Indeed, it was said that a retainer called Lightly led the murder of Edward II – at least, this was a local scholar's opinion. Mother accepted the theory with both shame and pleasure – as it has similarly confused me since.

But whatever the illicit grandeurs of her forebears, Mother was born to quite ordinary poverty, and was the only sister to a large family of boys, a responsibility she discharged somewhat wildly. The lack of sisters and daughters was something Mother always regretted; brothers and sons being her lifetime's lot.

Cider with Rosie by Laurie Lee,
First published in 1959

The real danger of writing constant summary is that you are giving your readers an 'infodump'. You're throwing facts at them and they will soon tire of blunt information unleavened by wit or style. Of course, you want to inform the reader about your life and possibly even your views and opinions, but what you don't want to do is to turn your story into a list of dull facts. A life story that reads like a bus time-table or a telephone directory will soon have the reader moving on, looking for a more satisfying read.

The problem lies, strangely enough, in the fact that, as writers, we are dealing with words. Our natural inclination is thus to think in terms of words. Whereas, what we should really be doing is thinking in terms of images, preferably moving ones, then looking for the words to match them.

Simply banging out an endless stream is not enough. The reader loses patience and is not gripped. We need to be able to make our readers 'see' the word picture that we have set out in front of them. This is why you need to write the following little phrase onto a piece of card and tape it to the frame of your computer monitor:

Show Don't Tell

'Show, don't tell' is the writer's mantra. Suppose you want to describe a person you once met. This person is called Arthur. He is a book-keeper. He is very nervous and has black hair. You could write:

Arthur was a book-keeper. He had black hair and was very nervous.

You've got all the facts in, but frankly, it's a bit dull. You are *telling* your readers about Arthur. You are doling out information. On the other hand, you can make it a little more interesting, by *showing* your readers this information, which will help them to visualise Arthur. You might write something like:

Arthur looked up from his accounts and pushed his black hair from his eyes with a trembling hand.

If Arthur is a more important character in your story, you might try something a little bit more complex:

At first sight, Arthur looked composed as he filled out the accounts book. His dark hair even lent him an air of seriousness. If you looked closer, the trembling hands showed that he was even more worried about redundancy than we were.

Similarly, in the following extract from the classic humour-travel book *Three Men in a Boat,* Jerome could simply tell us that Harris is incompetent, with no sense of direction and a misguided sense of his own knowledge and abilities. But he doesn't, what he writes is this account of Harris taking his cousin into Hampton Court Maze:

They met some people soon after they got inside, who said they had been there for three quarters of an hour, and had had about enough of it. Harris told them they could follow him if they liked; he was just going in, and then should turn round and come out again. They said it was very kind of him, and fell behind, and followed.

They picked up various other people who wanted to get it over, as they went along, until they absorbed all the persons in the maze. People who had given up all hopes of ever getting either in or out, or of ever seeing their home and friends again, plucked up courage, at the sight of Harris and his party, and joined the procession, blessing him. Harris said he should judge there must have been twenty people following him in all; and one woman with a baby, who had been there all morning, insisted on taking his arm, for fear of losing him.

Harris kept on turning to the right, but it seemed a long way, and his cousin said he supposed, it was a very big maze.

'Oh, one of the largest in Europe,' said Harris

'Yes, it must be,' replied the cousin, 'because we've walked a good two miles already.'

Harris began to think it rather strange himself, but he held on until, at last, they passed the half a penny bun on the ground that Harris's cousin swore he had noticed there seven minutes ago. Harris said: 'Oh, impossible!' but the woman with the baby said, 'Not at all,' as she herself had taken it from the child and thrown it down there just before she met Harris. She also added that she wished that she never had met Harris, and expressed an opinion that he was an impostor. That made Harris mad, and he produced his map, and explained his theory.

'That may maybe all right enough,' said one of the party, 'if you know whereabouts in it we are now.'

Harris didn't know, and suggested that the best thing to do would be to go back to the entrance, and begin again. For the beginning again part of it there was not much enthusiasm; but with regard to the advisability of going back to the entrance there was complete unanimity, and so they turned, and trailed after Harris again, in the opposite direction. About ten minutes more passed, and then they found themselves in the centre.

Harris thought at first of pretending that that was what he had been aiming at; but the crowd looked dangerous, and he decided to treat it as an accident.

Anyhow, they had got something to start from then. They did know where they were, and the map was once more consulted, and the thing seemed simpler than ever, and off they started for the third time.

And three minutes later they were back in the centre again.
Three Men in a Boat by Jerome K Jerome,
First published in 1889

Lack of space prevents me from giving you the conclusion of Harris's maze adventure and, whilst the prose is a little dated, you can see what I mean by showing rather than telling. We learn about Harris through his actions and those of the people around him. So, instead of writing a narrative summary (Harris once got badly lost at

Hampton Court Maze with a whole group of people), we get a full-blown picture.

This, in turn, leads us to the next aspect of writing that will help bring your words to life.

Writing in Scenes

If we follow our rule-of-thumb of 'show, don't tell', we can also place alongside it our second mantra 'write in scenes'. This too could be written on card and stuck to the side of your computer's monitor, but eventually you'll have more cards than screen.

Writing in scenes means that you need to think in terms of re-creating your life in more cinematic terms.

Let's imagine, you've jotted down the following:

Mother wanted me to get a job in an office, but I wanted to work outdoors. We argued about it, until eventually she let me go and work on Thompson's farm, where I knew there was a job going.

It's narrative summary, so it lacks the old 'show, don't tell', but it's also an opportunity missed. This is a scene. By merely summarising, you're missing the possibility of a touch of conflict. It's also the ideal place to try out a little dialogue, about which I'll say more later on in Chapter 8.

My mother raised her head from the Evening News. The quick crossword was half-finished.

'I've seen Bob Cox and he says there's a job going as a junior at Hetherington's'

'I'm not going to Hetherington's.' I put my bag on the table and took out the library books.

She sighed heavily, picked up the book from the top of the pile, turned it over and seemed to be reading the back. 'It's a good job. He says if you do well, then in a few months' time you can get day release.'

'Wow. You mean they'll let me out of the office one day a week?'

Her face said 'Don't take that tone with me.' Instead, she drew a deep breath and what she said was, 'It's got prospects. Play your cards right and they'll teach you to type.'

'I don't want to learn how to type.' Actually, I did. But I wanted to learn how to do other things as well.

'But typing's the future. In five or six years, you could even be a secretary.'

Five or six years? That was a third of a lifetime away. 'I'm not working cooped up in an office all day.'

We now have a scene that we can visualise, rather than just having pure facts relayed to us. It means that readers can empathize with the people involved, most especially the 'I', the person re-telling their story. We can put ourselves in her place. We've perhaps not had the exact same argument, but we've had disagreements with parents over what they want us to do and what we want to do - work, hobbies, girlfriends or boyfriends, owning a motorbike. And many of us have had arguments with our own children in our turn - work, hobbies, girlfriends, boyfriends, owning a motorbike ... and we will do down the generations. It is far more alive on the page than any bald statement written in narrative summary.

Start your scenes as near the end as you possibly can. In the example above, we don't see the narrator getting out the bicycle, pedalling to the library, locking the bike against the fence, furtling round the shelves, taking advice from the librarian ... blah, blah, we start with the confrontation that happens once the narrator gets home.

Over to You
Writing a scene

Look back at some of the notes you made at the end of the last chapter. See if you can spot an event that you think would make a great scene. Take the event and write it in scene form. Try to make what happens come alive for the reader.

When you've finished, read it over. Are there any places where you've got narrative summary, which might work better if it was written as a scene?

Remember: show, don't tell.

****

Chapter 6

Titles and Openings

Titles

Thinking of good titles is hard. I will admit that I always have tremendous difficulty. In fact, more than half of all the writing I've ever had published has had its title changed by an editor, publisher or producer. I've even resorted to internet chat sites to get other people to come up with the name for one of my plays.

It's up to you whether or not you want a title for each segment, section or chapter of your book (depending on how it's divided). If you want chapter titles, then you're actually creating quite a lot of work for yourself, although it does have the advantage of forcing you to think about the focus of each chapter.

In fact, for an over-arching title, you may feel that you don't need anything fancier than *Marmaduke Trembath – My Life* or *Gloria Gusset – Fifty Years in Knitwear*. However, unless you're particularly famous or intellectually lazy, in which case someone is probably ghost-writing your story anyway, then this kind of title is best used only if you're planning on handing out a few copies round friends and family.

Finding a good title is like panning for gold. But if you haven't got a title for your story when you begin, don't panic. You will think of something eventually or can resort to your Internet friends. You need to keep that notebook handy for the moment inspiration strikes. And it could strike anywhere. Yes, even in the loo. *Who's Afraid of Virginia Wolf* is supposedly a piece of graffiti that Edward Albee saw on a public lavatory wall. Although, if you have the same luck in a public loo, I suggest memorizing the graffiti and writing it down later, rather than being caught jotting notes in a public toilet.

There are several ways to come up with ideas. First of all, ask yourself what are the main themes of your book? Is there one part that seems to sum up your life? Is there a phrase that you've always liked that would serve as a title? Do you have a family saying? Or even a genuine family motto that's on your family crest (some people do). Is there a particular dictum you've always tried to live by (do unto others ...)?

You can always rely on the journalist's stock title-making mechanisms. These include:

- Finding an apt quotation. Dozens of books, films and plays use snippets of Shakespeare and other classics for their titles
- Borrowing a tile from another art form. Blake Morrison's *And When Did You Last See Your Father* is taken from the title of a famous painting by William Yeames in which a small child, obviously the son of a Cavalier, is questioned by Roundheads. Songs are often another source to be plundered. Might your autobiography carry a title such as *All Right Now* or *Top Hat, White Tie and Tails* or *Mad About the Boy* or *Teenage Kicks* or even, twisting titles from various sources in your tail of your Essex upbringing, *Don't Look Back in Ongar?*

- Using a well-known phrase or saying, then giving it a twist as we've just done above. *The Email of the Species Is More Deadly than the Mail* is one title I used some years ago for an article about the Internet when it was just taking off. It's a good title, though I confess I stole it, but I'm not going to say from whom

- Telling the public exactly what they're going to get - *A life in the Yorkshire Dales*. But be careful here; you can end up sounding a bit like poor old Gloria Gusset

- Extracting little phrases that you particularly like from your writing. But they have to be relevant and not just clever wordsmithery – that could look a bit pretentious

Finally, although there is no copyright on titles, and we've already seen that you are free to borrow them from the fine arts and music. But there's actually little point in using a well-known book title. *Wuthering Heights* by Arthur Johnson or *The Lord of the Rings* by Cynthia Harbottle are not going to fly off the shelves.

Writing Great Openings

How often have you opened a book in a bookshop or library, read the first few lines and either been hooked or turned off by what you read? I imagine there must be some people who will read anything, regardless of how awful those first few lines are, but most of us, I suspect, need to have our attention gripped from the start.

The beginning is the most important part of your story. It is vital that you write it well, so that your reader will carry on reading. A good opening doesn't have to be clever-clever, but it should intrigue us, hook us into the writer's world and make us read on to the next line and then the next and so on.

Every section you write - no matter how you choose to divide up your life story - needs to have a good strong opening. This is very hard to achieve. I've often used several of the examples that follow with students and had mixed reactions. Some of them have shown preferences for an opening line which others hated. This probably goes to show that you can't please all of the people all of the time. However, all the writers in this chapter are trying to achieve something with their openings, so the important thing is to try work out what kind of technique the author was using - what are they doing to try to make you read on? Is it a method you could adapt for your own use?

I fell in love with football as I was later to fall in love with women: suddenly, inexplicably, uncritically, giving no thought to the pain or disruption it would bring with it.
Fever Pitch by Nick Hornby,
First published in 1992

When I use this as an example, some students make the point that they're not interested in football, so probably wouldn't want to read on. This is fair enough. I don't buy books that have pink covers and I'd find it hard to read a book about motor-racing, pigeons or rattle-snake wrangling. We all have preferences. However, look beyond the football reference and you can see that this is a beautifully balanced opening line. It makes us want to know just how disastrous these love affairs are going to be. In what way is this all like football?

Note that Hornby uses the trick of a list of three items - *suddenly, inexplicably, uncritically.* The rule of three is a handy one for your tool-box. *Sex and drugs and rock and roll* is a much punchier line than having just two of the three items and if you add a fourth, you overload the idea. The rule of three is beloved of politicians *(liberté, égalité, fraternité)* and songwriters (*Bewitched, bothered and bewildered*) and religious leaders (*faith, hope and charity*) and next time you watch a comedian give out a list, notice that it is the third item that is funny. Now, here's Laurie Lee:

I was set down from the carrier's cart at the age of three; and there with a sense of bewilderment and terror my life in the village began.
Cider with Rosie by Laurie Lee,
First published in 1959

Of all the example openings I use, this is the one that gets the most praise. It's actually far less flamboyant than most of Lee's writing. What it does do is essentially say: this is where the story starts. He isn't going to pretend that he remembers much before the age of three and he's going to tell us about life in the little village. He's telling you straight what you're going to get. It's worth comparing it with Blake Morrison:

A hot September Saturday in 1959, and we are stationary in Cheshire. Ahead of us, a queue of cars stretches out of sight and round the corner. We haven't moved for ten minutes.
And When Did You Last See Your Father by Blake Morrison,
First published in 1993.

Here, Morrison seems to be doing something similar - giving us a situation, but he allows the reader to start posing more questions. A traffic jam in 1959? Did they even have them back then? It must have been something exceptional. Where are they going? Who are 'we'? Perhaps there's a touch more to intrigue us here: we sense something's going to happen. He's also not bothered to describe all the preparations needed to get into that traffic jam. He starts *in medias res* – in the middle of things.

With our next example, some people find the description tries just a little too hard. That's perhaps a matter of taste, but what Dave Eggers does here is to paint a scene.

Through the small tall bathroom window the December yard is grey and scratchy, the trees calligraphic. Exhaust from the dryer billows out of the house and up, breaking up while tumbling into a white sky.

The house is a factory.

A Heartbreaking Work of Staggering Genius by Dave Eggers,
First published in 2000

Some of his word choices are particularly striking - describing the trees as calligraphic is a masterstroke. Where many people come undone with this snippet is his description of the house as a factory. What is that supposed to mean? Is the house genuinely a factory? Are they drying so many clothes, that it's almost an industrial operation? Or is the house so ugly it could be confused for a factory? Is this very clever writing or, as several students have suggested, the writer trying it on and it doesn't mean anything? If you belong to the school of thought that says that you should call things what they are, then the idea of house as factory is fanciful tosh.

However, what you might also say about this piece is that it is all external. Although we're obviously getting the scene through Eggers's eyes, we're not really feeling anything. Hornby lays out his emotional stall, Lee tells of his childhood fears and Morrison is annoyingly stuck in a traffic jam. Eggers starts with a picture, so what about opening your life story with a snatch of dialogue?

'Marks!' yelled the guard. 'What's your number?'

'41526-004,' I mumbled, still in a really deep sleep. My number was used more often than my name and I knew it just as well.

Mr. Nice by Howard Marks,
First published in 1996

It's not the most elegantly written of our openings here, but using dialogue catapults you straight into the action. You want to know what's going on. Is he a soldier? In prison? If he's in prison, what has he done? What time of day is it that he's still in such a deep sleep?

What about using a bit of humour to start us off? Spike Milligan wrote a number of unreliable accounts of his war years and this is the opening to the first, and best, of these:

September 3rd, 1939. The last minutes of peace ticking away. Father and I were watching Mother digging our air-raid shelter. 'She's a great little woman,' said Father. 'And getting smaller

all the time,' I added. Two minutes later, a man called Chamberlain
who did Prime Minister impressions spoke on the wireless.
Adolf Hitler, My Part in his Downfall by Spike Milligan,
First published in 1971

This opening always gets a bit of a mixed reaction. There are the people who cry, 'I love Milligan' at the same time as others bow their heads and cry, 'I can't stand Spike Milligan.' So, again, as with the Nick Hornby example where the subject matter is football, a great deal of this may be down to taste.

I think this opening is tremendous. We know exactly where we are. Neither of the first two sentences starts with a verb, which is a trick Dickens used. You can see these two lazy grown men watching mother work. Then there is a surreal, visual gag about mother getting smaller all the time (as she disappears down the increasingly large hole - come on, keep up!) and the joke about Chamberlain is first rate. And then, we're catapulted straight into the Second World War. Most importantly, the tone of the book is set. We know that we're in comic territory. We bought this book, because we thought it would be funny and it's proving to be a good buy. I agree that if you don't get the humour, you probably won't get the book, but you can see how he sets out his stall very precisely.

Let's look at one last opening. It's another that often gets a mixed reaction. It's from Charles Bukowski's account of his years working for the American mail system.

It began as a mistake.
It was Christmas season and I learned from the drunk up
the hill, who did this trick every Christmas, that they would hire

damn near anybody, and so I went and the next thing I knew I had
this leather sack on my back and was hiking around at my leisure.
What a job, I thought. Soft!
Post Office by Charles Bukowski,
First published in 1971

Most people really like the first line. It begs the question 'What mistake was that?' They then feel that the second sentence could do with chopping in two. I tend to agree. What Bukowski is of course trying to do is to make his writing here seem like it's coming from the mouth of a man propping up the bar and telling his drinking companions a story. We also know that the job is going to be anything but soft. Jane Austen used an opening along these lines in a novel:

Emma Woodhouse, handsome, clever, and rich, with a
comfortable home and happy disposition, seemed to unite some of
the best blessings of existence; and had lived nearly twenty-one years
in the world with very little to distress or vex her.
Emma by Jane Austen,
First published in 1816

It's the same set-up – we're just waiting for Bukowski's job to prove a nightmare, in the same way as we know the rug is going to be pulled from underneath Emma's smug little feet.

So, when we're thinking about writing our opening sentence or two, we need to bear in mind the following. A good opening:

- interests the reader enough to make him or her read on (easier said than done)

- establishes the tone and mood of the piece you are writing. Is it serious or comic, conversational or literary, a read for the beach or one for the book group?
- sets up a 2-way relationship between reader and writer
- gives some kind of indication of what the subject matter is going to be and how the writer is going to deal with that subject matter

Obviously, there are as many ways to write openings as there are to write anything. However several common ways of writing them are:

- a simple declarative statement – *I've loved horses since I could first say the word*
- dialogue – *'You, my boy, are the laziest, rudest, messiest child that it has ever been my misfortune to teach,' said Mr. Shepherd*
- a surprising statement – *I'm the only person in our family who's still got their appendix*
- straight into the action - *I trained my telescopic sight on the man who seemed to be in charge*
- scene setting - *Our house was the only one in the street with a pink front door*

Make your reader ask themselves questions. Who is this person? Why are they doing that? Who's with them? Who are they talking to? Isn't that dangerous? Should she really be doing that in a speeding car? Isn't that illegal? Won't they get caught?

Intrigue them a little and they are much more likely to carry on reading. Bear in mind that you, the writer, are the only person who knows what happens next in your story. The reader has to read on to find out what it is you are going to say.

Don't forget that the great thing about modern technology is that word-processing means you can always write your first line at a later stage. So, if any good openings occur to you, jot them in your notebook and use them at a later stage.

Over to You

It won't take a genius to guess what little exercise I have for you at the end of this chapter. Spend ten minutes somewhere you can switch off all outside interference. It doesn't matter if it's by a stream, or in a café where you like the background hubbub or on the kitchen table whilst the vegetables are boiling. Then, take your notebook and simply write down sentences that you think might make a good opening line. It doesn't have to be for the very first page of your book, it can be for use at any point. Write down ten opening lines. Don't worry about how good they are, or if you're even going to use them. Simply write down ten starts. If you can do more, even better, but try for that as a minimum. Then, don't look at what you've written for at least a week.

When you come back to the list - are there any you can use or adapt? If you've come up with even one decent first line using this technique, then you've done well. Keep on doing the exercise until you've got enough great openings for all the section of your book.

Chapter 7

The People in Your Life

The people in our life story are its most important element. If you want another little slogan to add to the increasing number of little cards blu-tacked to the edge of your monitor, write down this one: people want to read about people. Yes, overseas locations, the way in which places have changed, or the workings of a submarine are fascinating. The building of the ring road and the demolishing of the windmill are interesting, but far more interesting is the colourful elderly lady who chained herself to the bulldozer when they came to build the road or the eccentric millionaire who'd made a dubious fortune and was rumoured to hold orgies by candle-light in the grain store. So this chapter is all about how we go about describing the people in our lives.

Describing People Using Narrative Summary

We looked at narrative summary in Chapter 5. There's nothing wrong with using it to describe people, but if you do use this technique then you want something a little more interesting than:

He was six foot tall and liked to wear a three-piece suit. In the garden, he grew roses and hydrangeas. He wasn't much of a drinker, but on Friday evenings he would go out at about nine o'clock and have a couple of pints and a game of dominos.

It's dull fare, so you would probably want to try to do it in a colourful way. Especially as sometimes, you may have no choice but to use narrative summary. It may be the case that all you have is a photograph. Perhaps you could think of writing something along the lines of Anna Funder's description of Erich Mielke, who was head of the East German secret police, the Stasi, for 30 years:

Photos show Mielke to be a small man with no neck. His eyes are set close together, his cheeks puffy. He has the face and the lips of a pugilist. He loved to hunt; footage shows him inspecting a line of deer carcasses as he would a military parade. He loved his medals, and wore them pinned over his chest in shiny noisy rows. He also loved to sing, mainly rousing marches and, of course, 'The Internationale'. It is said that psychopaths, people utterly untroubled by conscience, make supremely effective generals and politicians, and perhaps he was one. He was certainly the most feared man in the GDR; feared by colleagues, feared by Party members, feared by workers and the general population. 'We are not immune from villains among us,' he told a gathering of high-ranking Stasi officers in 1982. 'If I knew of any already, they wouldn't live past tomorrow. Short shrift. It's because I'm a humanist that I am of this view.' And, 'all this blithering about to execute or not to execute, for the death penalty or against – all rot, comrades. Execute! And, when necessary, without a court judgment.'

Stasiland by Anna Funder,
First published in 2003

This is a neat tight description and we immediately get an idea of what Mielke was like. You certainly wouldn't want to get on the wrong side of him. She follows it up with a brief résumé of Mielke's life and crimes. All this is part of the background information Funder needs to lay out before she can tell us a great deal more about the workings of the Stasi, one of the most ruthless secret police forces of any era.

When using narrative summary, you need to bring in some colour. This is what David Sedaris does in the following extract in which he describes his dreamy sister and, importantly, the way in which he feels he'd have liked to have been something like her in terms of temperament and character:

At an early age my sister Gretchen exhibited a remarkable talent for drawing and painting. Her watercolours of speckled mushrooms and bonneted girls were hung with pride in the family room, and her skill was encouraged with private lessons and summer visits to sketching camp. Born with what my mother described as an 'artistic temperament', Gretchen floated from blossom to blossom in a blissful haze. Staring dreamily up at the sky, she tripped over logs and stepped out in front of speeding bicycles. When the casts were placed on her arms and legs, she personalised them with Magic Marker daisies and fluffy clouds. Physically she'd been stitched up more times than the original flag, but mentally nothing seemed to touch her. You could tell Gretchen anything in strict confidence, knowing that five minutes later she would recall nothing but the play of shadows on your face. It was like having a foreign-exchange student living in our house. Nothing we did our said made any sense to her, as she seemed to follow the rules and customs of some

exotic, faraway nation where citizens drilled the ground for oil paint and picked pastels from the branches of stunted trees. Without copying anyone else, she had invented her own curious personality, which I envied more than her artistic ability.
Me Talk Pretty One Day by David Sedaris,
First published in 2000

Sedaris digs a little deeper than the surface of his sister. He could say she's dreamy. Instead, she 'floated from blossom to blossom in a blissful haze'. He gives us an idea of the kinds of pictures she painted - 'speckled mushrooms and bonneted girls'. Instead of saying she is accident-prone and leaving it at that, he involves her in tripping over logs and walking into speeding bicycles, but importantly, she then decorates her plaster casts. Instead of giving us a litany of her disasters, he uses a couple of examples. And when he looks for some way of summing her up, he describes her as being like 'a foreign exchange student living in our house.'

I reiterate that any chunk of narrative summary should be kept short, made as colourful as possible and as soon as possible we should get back into show-mode, rather than tell-mode.

How Much Do We Need to Know about the People in Your Story?

It's also a common beginners' mistake to give us a wodge of information about a new character the moment that character is introduced. Harder to do, but much more satisfying both for the reader, and for your sense of achievement as a writer, is to drip feed the information that we need about a character into the course of your tale.

Another danger of narrative summary is that we get purely static description. We paint a word picture of the person, but it is like a still photograph rather than a film.

Writing about one of the people in your life as they go about some task is far more rewarding. That task doesn't have to be anything particularly esoteric, either. I have read brilliant character descriptions of grannies baking, younger brothers assembling and disassembling mopeds in the kitchen sink, fathers putting up rickety shelving and sisters getting ready for a night out. One of the best descriptions I ever read was of buying a 45 rpm single and taking it home and putting it on the record-player. It's not always in the big events of life that we reveal our characters to the world.

For example, if your mother was a stickler for neatness and cleanliness, you might write something like this:

Mother had spent the first decade of married life in army quarters. Every time they moved house, which was often, they would be subjected to the 'white glove inspection' of their army-provided housing.

Some junior officer or NCO, with little to keep him busy in a peace-time army, would be dispatched to the house to inspect every wall, surface and ceiling for the slightest sign of dilapidation. Anything wrong and the cost was deducted from Dad's pay.

Paintwork must be scratch-free, windows diamond-bright, skirting-boards must show not the slightest mark of a clumsy, passing boot. Finally, the inspector would snap on a pair of virginal white cotton gloves and run a suspicious finger over fixtures and fittings. Dust was the final enemy.

As a result, mother had adopted a military routine to tidying and cleaning the house. Feather duster tucked like a swagger-stick under one arm, she marshalled abandoned dinky toys, lonely slippers and building blocks into serried ranks on the kitchen table.

Bobby pins and Kirkby grips, Action Man's leg or stray bubble-gum cards of Mickey Dolenz would be squadroned according to whom she had decided was their owner. And, oh, the humiliation of being the one with the most articles on that table.

Next came the blitzkrieg on the sitting-room. Dad's easy-chair was body-searched for stray change that might have fallen down the loose covers tucked into its sides and back.

Spiders were driven from their homelands, their cobwebs razed as Mother swept away all that lay before her. Like the cavalry, mother showed no quarter.

But, despite the military precision of her cleaning, there was always the cigarette, jammed and jiggling at the corner of her mouth.

Notice the weight of military imagery and vocabulary that is used in that description:

Swagger stick ... marshalled ... squadroned ... blitzkrieg ... body-searched ... driven from their homelands ...razed ... cavalry ... no quarter.

Using words like these brings the scene alive in the reader's mind. Yet nothing else has happened except that she has tidied up the house. There's also a spattering of cultural allusions here - Bobby pins, Kirkby grips, Action Man, Mickey Dolenz - which help give the piece a sense of time and place.

Knowing the People in Your Story

One of the hardest parts of telling any story - real or imagined - is how much information we want to get across about the person concerned.

Sometimes, you can fall into the trap of thinking that the reader needs to know absolutely everything. But this isn't the case. As I stated earlier, readers are perfectly capable of filling in the gaps, so they don't need to know every little detail. After all, you don't know everything about that person. Let's face it, it's impossible to know everything that there is to know about anybody. We don't even know ourselves totally. We don't know what other people think about us and as we forget large chunks of what we have done; we're an incomplete portrait of ourselves even in our own heads. Readers will join the dots, they will colour in the remainder of the portrait. You, the writer, have to decide how much the reader needs to know.

'How much is that?' you ask.

Well, frankly, there's no good answer. However, common sense would dictate that if your granny is only a passing character in your story and your father is pivotal, we probably need to know a lot less about her than about him. And do we really need to know your father's shoe size, unless of course he was a size sixteen, in which case that's pretty interesting.

When writing about the people in your story, you may find it useful to jot down a few notes about that person. Here is a list of the kinds of things you might like to think about:

- Name, including nicknames or family names. Any titles they might have used

- Age or age span during the course of your book, or at the time of the events you are describing. Perhaps importantly, their age as related to you
- Date of birth – what else happened that year? Can we place people in the context of the world they grew up in?
- Place of birth – what's the place like? Has it changed since then? Has it gentrified or become a slum? What kind of social milieu was this? Were times easy or hard? The kind of house they live(d) in. Messy? Spotless? Huge? Tiny?
- Height, weight, colour of hair and eyes. Did they have any distinguishing features - perhaps scars or some kind of physical handicap?
- Habits and mannerisms. Way of speaking – e.g. Gentle and slow? Sharp and with a strong local accent? Precisely and in Received Pronunciation? Did they have any pet sayings?
- Job(s). Did they enjoy work? Did they achieve their ambitions?
- Brothers & sisters, their place in family (e.g. eldest child)
- Education
- Friends, enemies?
- Skills, strengths and weaknesses
- Interests
- Taste in music, films, television, art, theatre

What other information do you want us to know about this person? It might be worth looking back to Chapter 2, where there is a list of questions that you might want to ask yourself about your own life and see if they might be relevant here.

Even if you managed to scrape together all the information to be able to answer all of the above questions, you are unlikely to pass it on wholesale to the reader. However, it's the kind of note-taking that will help you to focus on the person about whom you are writing.

Over to You

Read this thumbnail sketch of the Belgian cyclist Eddy Merckx as he was several years after his great cycling successes.

Nowadays Eddy Merckx is rotund to the point of globularity. Putting on weight is a problem for the retired pro cyclist. Riding burns up a lot of energy, and they eat accordingly; chomping down a 3,500-calorie breakfast is a hard habit to break. Once they slip off the saddle for the final time many bike-racers balloon up as if someone has just pulled the rip-cord on a life-jacket beneath their shirt.

Despite the change in shape Merckx was easily recognisable. He still has the wide sharkish smile and those eyelashes. Merckx's eyelashes are easily the longest and most luxuriant in the history of the sport. Even Betty Boop envies Eddy's eyelashes.

Merckx's mastery of his sport was complete. He was the Bradman of the bicycle. Like the Don, he ruled with a combination of iron will and skill, and a dash of the sort of cunning that would have put a grin on the face of Niccolo Machiavelli. In 1996 King Albert II made Eddy a Baron, presumably on the grounds that a country with a bicycling monarchy needs a bicycling aristocracy to go with it. Baron, with its connotations of swagger and the brutal exercising of power, is the perfect prefix for Eddy Merckx...

...There is a myth is sport about 'the hungry fighter'. Merckx was from a comfortable middle-class background, yet he had a formidable will to win. An American football coach once taunted a less successful rival with the comment, 'The trouble with your guys is they all have their own teeth.' In this dental index of competitiveness, Merckx makes Nobby Stiles look like the Osmonds.

A Tall Man in a Low Land by Harry Pearson,
First published in 2000

Now think about someone from your past. Write a description of them in around 300 words. Try to keep your vocabulary imaginative (*round to the point of globularity*) and to make sure that we learn something about the person's appearance as well as their attitudes.

****

Chapter 8

An Ear for Dialogue

Dialogue often seems a frightening proposition for a life-writer. Nick Hornby sums up one major dilemma. Here, he speaks (as a youngster) to the footballer Bob McNab, who has been out of the Arsenal first team for four months with an injury:

> *'Are you playing, Bob?'*
>
> *'Yeah.'*
>
> *Dialogue in works of autobiography is quite naturally viewed with some suspicion. How on earth can a writer remember verbatim conversations that happened fifteen, twenty, fifty years ago? But 'Are you playing, Bob?' is one of only four sentences I have ever uttered to any Arsenal player. For the record the others are 'How's the leg, Bob?' to Bob Wilson, recovering from injury the following season; 'Can I have your autograph, please?' to Charlie George, Pat Rice, Alan Ball and Bertie Mee; and, well, 'How's the leg, Brain?' to Brian Marwood outside the Arsenal club shop when I was old enough to know better and I can therefore vouch for its absolute authenticity.*
>
> *Fever Pitch by Nick Hornby,*
> *First published in 1992*

This neatly sums up our fear of dialogue. How can anyone remember exactly what old Arthur said to them? That was fifty years ago! The truth is that they didn't remember precisely what he said. You may be able to remember one or two things verbatim - the time your teacher picked on you for no apparent reason or the time your boss told you you were the best thing since sliced bread. But, in reality, most of us have fuzzy memories about what people have said to us over the years.

You are allowed a little licence. And the reason you're allowed it is because a life story that contains no dialogue is likely to be very stodgy indeed. In fact, I'd go out on a limb and suggest it will probably be unreadable. So, you're allowed a little latitude to reconstruct conversations. Although there are caveats with writing speech, of which we'll have more later, there are several good reasons to do so.

When you write dialogue, the people in your story are actually doing something. They are speaking. When they speak, they move your story along, add interest by how they speak and help you keep to the mantra of 'show don't tell'. Using dialogue helps you to write in scenes, rather than just doling out factual information.

Readers also tend to like dialogue. They like to conjure up the voices in their heads. This means that they are bringing something of themselves to the experience of reading.

Speech also helps to break up the page visually. It creates white space - essentially the bits of the printed page that don't have print on them. This makes it much easier for the eye to follow, especially as it's likely you'll be printing out your finished copy on A4 paper. White space is good. If you're not sure, just think of how off-putting a page of entirely blocked text can be. And if that doesn't convince you, print out an A4 page of paragraph-free text and see how you like the look of that!

The Function of Dialogue

Dialogue in life writing can also perform many of the same important narrative functions that it does in works of fiction:

- to give information
- to reveal emotion
- to advance the story
- to build character

Let's look at each in turn...

To Give Information

If you're using this technique, you need to be quite subtle. The information needs to come across naturally, as part of your story. If you simply put information into a person's mouth so as to avoid writing in the narrative, it can ring false. It's easy enough to write this sort of infodump disguised as speech:

'Edwina, you are my cousin and as the daughter of my mother's brother, you have meant a lot to me ever since we were both struck by lightning when we had that holiday in Greece together and both caught a stomach bug. Then you had to go to hospital ...'

... the result is appalling, I trust you agree. Both Edwina and the speaker know all this, so why are they telling each other?

In an effort to avoid one person doling out information, you might want to split it between two people. The danger then is that you fall into a slightly different trap and that is one of writing ping-pong dialogue. In this case, two people merely swap information, every subject is over- introduced as though in big neon signs and you often end up with a stilted question/answer session as in the following:

'I understand you're not happy at work.'
'That's true.'
'Is it your boss?'
'Yes.'
'What is it about him?'
'He expects me to do too much.'
'What kinds of things does he expect you to do?'
'Oh, work late, do unpaid overtime, that kind of thing.'

If all your dialogue ends up sounding like a lawyer's cross-examination, then you're not going to grab the reader. In this instance, we still have the problem that the people in your tale are telling each other information they already know.

Often, if you just want the reader to know a piece of information, rather than trying to force it into someone's mouth, falling back on plain old-fashioned narrative summary does the job:

Mrs. Smith had worked at Jones and Jones since before the Great War.

To Reveal Emotion

This is quite subtle to achieve, but here's a bit from Edmund White's *A Boy's Own Story* to illustrate what I mean. The narrator has just finished a phone call and runs in to see his mother, who is sewing on a button:

> *'Guess what!' I shouted.*
>
> *'What, dear?' She licked the thread and tried again.*
>
> *'That was Tom and he arranged a date for me with Helen Paper, who's the most sophisticated girl in the whole school.'*
>
> *'Sophisticated?' There, the thread had gone through.*
>
> *'Yes, yes' - I could hear my voice rising higher and higher; somehow I had to convey the excitement of my prospects - 'she's only a freshman but she goes out with college boys and everything and she's been to Europe and she's - well, the other girls say top-heavy but only from sour grapes. And she's the leader of the Crowd or could be if she cared and didn't have such a reputation.'*
>
> *A Boy's Own Story by Edmund White,*
> *First published in 1982*

See how anxious the narrator is to please his mother - in fact, he's trying to persuade both himself and her that he's not gay, hence the excitement of a date with a girl. And a girl with large breasts at that. Notice also that his mother says so little, that we can only assume that she's not really interested in him. That one word of dialogue spoken by his mother 'Sophisticated?' carries a huge amount of weight.

To Advance Your Story

This can be quite complex, but here's one simple way to use it:

> 'We're moving to Germany,' my father announced one morning at breakfast.

You could also argue that this gives us information. Good, this is dialogue performing more than one function (as with the extract from Edmund White above).

To Build Character

Characters can say things that reveal information about themselves and other characters. How people speak also reveals a good deal about them.

The Edmund White extract tells us a great deal about the mother's indifference to her son and his desperate attempts to cover up his homosexuality.

Ideally a speech (and its context) should perform at least two of these four narrative functions:

> 'We're moving to Germany,' my father announced one morning at breakfast.
> 'Over my dead body.' My mother moved the milk jug out of his reach.

Think about what this short exchange does. Why does it carry much more weight by being in dialogue?

Naturalistic Dialogue

People rarely speak the Queen's English and this should be reflected in contractions, such as *haven't, wouldn't, couldn't, gonna* (no matter what your primary school teacher taught you). You have to make your dialogue sound like people talking. This is easier to say than it is to do.

Make what people say too stilted and grammatical, and it won't sound like speech. It'll sound like some kind of textbook. On the other hand, if you were to copy the exact way in which people talk, it would be too much. Real speech is full of ums and errs, repeated statements, half-finished sentences. In real life, we are a mass of hesitations and speech tics. We start a sentence seeming to be talking about one thing, change our minds part-way through and end up talking about something else. Most annoyingly of all, when we speak, we don't do punctuation. You'll get exchanges like this:

A. *It's me ... you all right, cause ... she came over ... but ... the thing's not there, you know*

B. *No... yeah ... no, fine ... it's, you know, sorted ... he was like ...*

A. *I might not ...*

B. *No. Me too. I'm not sure ... I think ... well ... I'm not sure.*

No, we've got no idea what it's about. It could be anything. When we write dialogue, we just need to give it a flavour of real speech, without necessarily going the whole way. However, when you're trying to make everything sound natural, you may find you end up with a tendency to write dialogue that takes us nowhere in particular, but sounds like people talking:

Man: What's on the menu tonight?
Barman: We've got sausages, lasagne, scampi, liver and bacon.
Man: What kind of sausages are they?
Barman: They're Lincolnshire sausages, as you're asking.
Man: The lasagne is it beef or lamb?
Barman: Beef.
Man: Mmm. Good, I like beef.

If you find you've written anything like this (and we all do), then cross it out when you get to editing stage and stick to dialogue that tells us the story or tells us about character.

Dialect

You also need to make a decision about local accents and dialect. There's no hard and fast rule on this one, but unless your book is going to have a very limited local appeal, it's probably best to cut dialect as such to a minimum. You can sound condescending and you may end up writing something that is unintelligible to the reader:

Ahv garn orf 'em strechlin' udder dingtops as they wus allus in the mood for a-brekkin'

However, there are some aspects of speech that can be found in all sorts of different dialects. Words such as 'gotta', 'wanna' or 'cos', for 'got to', 'want to' and 'because' are commonly used. Many people, when they speak, lose the ends of words - *doin'* for *doing*, or fail to aspirate the letter H - *'ouse* for *house*.

There is no reason why you can't use a sprinkling of these words to show that someone is speaking in dialect, but be careful. Whilst we may understand these words easily when they are spoken, they're sometimes very hard to follow when written on the page.

If you want to indicate a strong regional accent, you can always write something along the lines of:

'I'm not doing it, and that's that,' he said in his strong Yorkshire accent.

The advantage of this is that the reader can do their own Yorkshire accent in their head, and whilst you may be able to distinguish Hull from Bradford, and Leeds from the Dales, it actually doesn't matter to the reader. The accent in the their head is good enough, even if it's nearer rural Lancashire or BBC multi-purpose Northern, or even Gloucestershire than the Yorkshire dialect you were writing.

A further way of indicating dialect is by the use of grammar that is typical of speech rather than the written word. In order to be grammatically correct, we might write 'He was sitting on a chair'. However, your character might say, 'He was sat on a chair.'

If you have to use words that are specifically local, you can either explain them in the text or even use an asterisk and give a 'translation' in the footer of the page. If you are using an extensive number of local or specialised words, then it might even be worthwhile putting together a short glossary. My inclination would be to have this somewhere at the front of the book, rather than at the back, so that the reader spots it before he or she gets into the main body of your work

You can also use phrases (provided they aren't clichéd) to give the 'spirit' of the region:

'You missed your bus? That's too bad.'

'You missed your bus? Well, duck, hop in. I'll give you a lift'.

Or you can simply write:

'Good morning, campers,' she said in a strong Birmingham accent.

Writing good dialogue is hard, but don't be afraid of it. And remember it doesn't have to come in vast swathes, even the occasional bit of speech spices up your writing.

Over to You

Some people find dialogue really difficult to write. If you are one of these people, try the following little exercise.

Take an episode from your life that involved you and one other person. An argument, an interview or some kind of confrontation often works well for this.

Write the episode purely in dialogue – almost like the script for a radio play. Lay it aside for a few days. When you read it again, are there any bits that could be cut to keep the dialogue good and punchy? Cut them out, and then add in some narrative flesh to give your dialogue some context.

****

Chapter 9

Writing about Places

Writing descriptions of places we know is one of the skills that most of us were taught in English lessons at school. As a result, we feel fairly confident that we can do it. And we probably can. The danger with description lies not in the fact that we can do it, but in the fact that it is so easy to overdo it.

A little over 100 years ago, few people had ventured more than a couple of miles from the place they were born. Their visual vocabulary was limited to the world that immediately surrounded them. If you worked in an industrial town, chances were you lived there as well. The landscape of your mind would be that of factories, high-density housing and the occasional oasis of green in the middle of a bustling city.

Conversely, country-dwellers might never leave the valley where they lived and worked. Everything they needed to sustain everyday existence would be at hand: food came from the land they worked, clothes and the tools of their trades were made at home or by local specialist tradesmen and women.

Holidays within the shores of this country were a luxury even for the new, burgeoning middle-classes. Holidays abroad were almost exclusively for the rich. Sailors and soldiers were the most frequent travellers. A journey to India took weeks, not a few hours.

Cheap, fast travel, newspapers and magazines, the cinema, and most importantly of all, television, have changed our horizons, opening up new vistas to all of us. Each of us now has an encyclopaedic visual vocabulary that three generations ago would have been way beyond the furthest fringes of the imagination of the most prescient and intrepid traveller.

Nowadays, click on your TV set (and you don't even have to travel across the room to do that, because you've got a remote control) and you can be transported almost anywhere. On one channel there is an adventure movie featuring an Alpine ravine. Another channel has a travelogue showing sun-drenched beaches in Bali. Another has a documentary showing us the grimmest Buenos Aires slums.

This increasingly visual personal database means that we see the world not in terms of words, but in terms of images. The net effect for you as a writer is that your audience, in general, feels less need for long descriptions. It may be fair enough for Thomas Hardy to write 17 pages showing us the contours of Egdon Heath, but the modern reader has little patience for that. Some might argue it is because our attention spans have been weakened by the evil forces of television and hand-held devices; others that we simply don't need the volume of description because somewhere in our memory banks we have pictures that will illustrate a scene for our own purposes. Whatever the reason, we don't need that level of description, because with just a few well-chosen words on the part of the author, we 'get the picture'.

It is extremely easy to bore your reader with excessive description. It is also very easy for you to get carried away when you are writing it. As majestic phrases tumble from your pen, you feel it is your bounden duty to record them for your readership. Just remember, that reader may soon lose patience. Sometimes, less is more.

Let's take that 'Alpine Ravine' of a couple of paragraphs back as an example. I suspect that those two words were all you needed to summon up a picture to your mind.

On the other hand, it is perfectly reasonable to say a little more about it. For instance:

We found ourselves on the edge of a ridge. The mountain fell away below us almost vertically. It was the kind of place where even the most seasoned climber would feel a knot of tension developing in his stomach. In the ravine, the winter snows had already begun to melt revealing the tops of harsh, black rocks, many the size of a small house.

It's worth noting a few of things about this little description.

First, there are people in the scene. In this case it is 'we', although the reader, from this tiny snippet, doesn't learn a great deal more about who 'we' are. Peopling your landscape adds interest for the reader. Perhaps we're going to find out who 'we' are later, or maybe we already know.

Second, there is a sense of movement in the piece. All that happens is that we walk to a ridge and look down. However, that means that what we are getting is a moving image of the scene, rather than a still photograph.

Third, there is an emotional tone to the description. In this case, it is something to do with the fear/anxiety/nervousness of looking into a sheer drop.

Put people into your descriptions and have them do things and I guarantee that your writing will be ten times better than using the still camera approach to description.

Description Doesn't Have To Be Beautiful

I suspect that when we see a beautiful landscape, we might want to recapture that in words. But writing about places doesn't mean that you have to like them. Description is also very powerful when we are writing about something unpleasant. Indeed giving somewhere a good kicking is a staple in the genre of travel writing.

In the following extract, Jerome K. Jerome lets rip briefly about the town of Maidenhead.

Maidenhead itself is too snobby to be pleasant. It is the haunt of the river swell and his overdressed female companion. It is the town of showy hotels, patronized chiefly by dudes and ballet girls. It is the witch's kitchen from which go forth those demons of the river - steam launches. The London Journal duke always has his 'little place' at Maidenhead; and the heroine of the three-volume novel always dines there when she goes out on the spree with somebody else's husband.

Three Men in a Boat by Jerome K Jerome,
First published in 1889

I apologise to anyone from Maidenhead and only hope the place has improved, but this is a wonderful, quick kicking. How much more satisfactory to write something like this than to have a go at a person from one's past.

Jenny Diski in her travel memoir *Stranger on a Train*, in which she tours the United States by rail is also less than impressed by Old Sacramento, which she describes as 'new, but distressed Sacramento', hating the fakery that has gone into recreating part of the town as a tourist attraction:

You clattered along the boarded, porched sidewalks complete with horse-retaining rails, but entered bright air-conditioned emporia selling cheap, tatty replicas of items that were once desirable mainly for their practicality: durable hats, boots, leather bags for cowboys to improve their peripatetic existence, now remodelled in shoddy materials and badly but equally suitably made for the life they would lead in the backs of wardrobes. Subsistence supplies had changed, too. Barrels of flour were replaced by Perspex containers keeping popcorn warm. A slug of whisky was more likely to be a Tequila Sunrise. A lunch of just-off-the-hoof steak with beans became toasted goat's cheese and oakleaf salad. Old Sacramento turned out to be themed streets of tourist shops. Heritage with fries. But signs (done as old 'Wanted' posters) boasted proudly of the restoration of the deteriorated and decayed 'historical district', at the sweeping away of the inner-city blight and the reclaiming of the past for the edification of visitors. Of course, the past was not so much reclaimed as sanitised and sold, and it is startling how quickly these bright new versions of history become tawdry, as the gilding wears off and reveals the paper-thin profit motive. Apparently, if you tidy things up in order to sell crap, the crap wins out.
Stranger on a Train by Jenny Diski,
First published in 2002

Notice how Diski uses movement in this piece to lift it. Words like 'clattered' do an awful lot of work as do other verbs such as 'decayed', 'sweeping', 'sanitised and sold'. Even a phrase such as 'the gilding wears off' implies movement, or at least change, which make the whole description livelier. It also allows you to go further than you can with a photograph, where the surface might hide what lies beneath.

Atmosphere

Atmosphere is one of those horribly vague words. It's hard to define what we mean by it, but we know when we read something that lacks it: what we're reading just isn't enjoyable.

If you enter an eerie, creepy, derelict building, we want to feel your fear and nervousness alongside you. We want to know that your breath hangs in the cold night air, that your legs are trembling, that you feel sick to your stomach. If you don't conjure up a word picture that takes us there, then there is no atmosphere. We want to live your life alongside you.

Similarly, if you are describing a scene from the markets of Marrakech, then we don't just want to know what it looks like. We want to know all about the sounds and the smells. What do the hawkers shout? When you stop for a coffee what does it taste like? Strong and bitter? Milky and sweet?

As a writer, you create atmosphere by using a variety of techniques and one of the most common ways is by adding sensory description to your writing.

There are, of course, five senses – sight, sound, smell, touch and taste. It would take a truly astounding writer to be able to create atmosphere by appealing to just one of those senses. However, often when we start out as writers, we ignore the fact that we can appeal to five different senses and tend to concentrate on just one – sight.

I'm not going to suggest that every time you write a descriptive passage you include something that appeals to all the senses. In fact, if you do, you'll find it's rather like making a currant cake only to find that all the fruit has globbed together in a lump. It's too rich.

However, if you do write bearing in mind that you want to appeal to more than just the sense of sight, then you will find that your writing is vastly improved for it.

Let me show you what I mean.

Writing using just 'sight':

I saw the old man from the corner of my eye. I tried hard not to look at him – with his dirty clothes and matted hair.

Yes, we see the dirty clothes and matted hair, but to be honest, we're not getting much, and we're certainly not getting that magic ingredient atmosphere.

So let's try again, using all five senses:

I caught sight of the old man from the corner of my eye. He wore tatty, dirty clothes that reeked like stale cabbage even at twenty paces. As the old man moved towards me, the smell grew stronger, almost overwhelming, until I could feel the first rush of water in my mouth that signalled I was going to be sick. The old man reached out a quivering hand, its fingernails long and blackened with soil and touched my face. His hand was sandpaper on my face – rough, harsh, unforgiving. My heart drummed a tattoo in my chest.

Sight – the tatty, dirty clothes

Smell – the reek of stale cabbage

Taste – the rush of water

Touch – the sandpapery hand

Sound – the drumming (also perhaps 'touch'?)

You'll see that by cramming in all five senses I've overdone it a bit, but I'm sure you get the point. We're now alongside the narrator, wondering what is going to happen to him next.

I've even seen the piece of advice that you should take a different colour highlighter pen for each of the senses (e.g. pink for smell, yellow for taste) and when you've finished writing go through with each colour and mark up which senses you've used. That way you can see if you are writing genuinely sensuous prose.

It's such a simple technique. Bring several of the senses to your writing and you will find that you will quickly draw in that sixth sense – atmosphere.

It's what Dylan Thomas achieves in the following little extract:

August Bank Holiday - a tune on an ice-cream cornet. A slap of sea and a tickle of sand. A fanfare of sunshades opening. A wince and whinny of bathers dancing into deceptive water. A tuck of dresses. A rolling of trousers. A compromise of paddlers. A sunburn of girls and a lark of boys. A silent hullabaloo of balloons. Holiday Memory by Dylan Thomas, First published in 1954.

Note how Thomas relies mainly on sounds linked to images to bring to life a bank holiday by the sea, although some of the combinations of images appeal to more than one sense - a tune played on an ice-cream cornet appeals to sight, taste and sound, and also carries the extra weight of the word-play.

If you enjoyed this little snippet, then you'll want to read more. Be aware that it's a difficult trick to pull off a piece of writing quite like this, but what is interesting is the way in which you get the scene on the beach immediately, even down to the seediness of the slap and tickle that smacks of Donald McGill postcards. Some of you, however, might find this writing a bit rich and likely to give you full-blown indigestion. If you're more prosaic, then attempting to stretch this far might just result in purple prose, or be downright pretentious.

Over to You
Cider with Rosie by Laurie Lee

Look at this passage from Laurie Lee's acclaimed memoir of village life as we're going cherry-pick it for some of the lessons it can teach us:

The day was over and we had used it, running errands or prowling the fields. When evening came we returned to the kitchen, to its smoky comfort, in from the rapidly cooling air to its wrappings of warmth and cooking. We boys came first, scuffling down the bank, singly, like homing crows. Long tongues of shadows licked the curves of the fields and the trees turned plump and still. I had been off to Painswick to pay the rates, running fast through the long wet grass, and now I was back, panting hard, the job finished, with hay seeds stuck to my legs. A plate of blue smoke hung above our chimney, flat in the motionless air, and every stone in the path as I ran down home shook my bones with arriving joy.

We chopped wood for the night and carried it in; dry beech sticks as brittle as candy. The baker came down with a basket of bread slung carelessly over his shoulder. Eight quartern loaves, cottage-size, black crusted, were handed in at the door. A few crisp flakes of pungent crust still clung to his empty basket, so we scooped them up on our spit-wet fingers and laid them upon our tongues. The twilight gathered, the baker shouted goodnight, and whistled his way up the bank. Up in the road his black horse waited, the cart lamps smoking red.

Indoors, our Mother was cooking pancakes, her face aglow from the fire. There was a smell of sharp lemon and salty batter, and the burning hiss of oil. The kitchen was dark and convulsive with shadows, no lights had yet been lit. Flames leapt, subsided, corners woke and died, fires burned in a thousand brasses.

'Poke around for the matches, dear boy,' said Mother 'Damn me if I know where they got to.'

We lit the candles and set them about, each in its proper order: two on the mantelpiece, one on the piano, and one on a plate in the window. Each candle suspended a ball of light, a luminous fragile glow, which swelled and contracted to the spluttering wick or leaned to the moving air. Their flames pushed weakly against the red of the fire, too tenuous to make much headway, revealing our faces more by casts of darkness than by any clear light they threw.

Cider with Rosie by Laurie Lee,
First published in 1959

Now look back over this little extract noting all the different senses that Lee uses as he describes the kitchen of the family cottage. If this is a library book, don't use marker pens!

Sight:

Sound:

Touch:

Taste:

Smell:

Then go through the piece and write down the verbs (doing words) that Lee uses to add movement and depth to the piece.

Lastly, does this piece appeal to you, or do you find it a bit too rich?

The World of Work

You are almost sure to write something about your work. Workplaces have changed remarkably over the years and here's one from Charles Dickens that depicts a pretty unsavoury factory in the early part of the 19th Century. You have to hope that workplaces like this don't exist anymore, but I fear that they do, even if not necessarily in the UK. As you read it, it's worth bearing in mind what I said earlier - that that description doesn't always have to be about pretty things. Charles Dickens's childhood was not the easiest, but provided him with plenty of material including a spell working at a blacking warehouse as a young boy.

The Blacking-warehouse was the last house on the left-hand side of the way, at old Hungerford stairs. It was a crazy, tumble-

down old house, abutting the river, and literally overrun with rats. Its wainscoted rooms and its rotten floors and staircase, and the old grey rats swarming down in the cellar, and the sound of their squeaking and scuffling coming up the stairs at all times, and the dirt and decay of the place, rise up visibly before me, as if I were there again. The counting-house was on the first floor, looking over the coal-barges and the river. There was a recess in it, in which I was to sit and work. My work was to cover the pots of paste-blacking; first with a piece of oil-paper, and then with a piece of blue paper; to tie them round with a string; and then to clip the paper close and neat, all round, until it looked as smart as a pot of ointment from an apothecary's shop. When a certain number of grosses of pots had attained this pitch of perfection, I was to paste on each a printed label; and then go on again with more pots. Two or three other boys were kept at similar duty downstairs on similar wages. One of them came up, in a ragged apron and paper cap, on the first Monday morning, to show me the trick of using the string and tying the knot. His name was Bob Fagin; and I took the liberty of using his name long afterwards, in Oliver Twist.

Autobiographical Fragment by Charles Dickens,
First published 1847

Notice that Dickens uses plenty of actions - we see young David actually physically doing things - which helps to stop the description from being too static, even if the sentence length in a couple of places is a bit long for modern tastes.

Now it's your turn. Write about a place you have worked or know well and try to bear in mind some of the techniques discussed in this chapter: appealing to different senses, having people in your description, getting in some movement, using good, strong verbs. Above all, by using these little techniques see if you can conjure up some atmosphere.

****

Chapter 10

Adding a Pinch More Spice

In this chapter, we're going to look at some other techniques that can help enliven your writing. They're a bit of a mixed bag, but nonetheless important all the same.

Conflict

A story is not a story without some kind of conflict. Without conflict, what you write will be a bloodless, lifeless limp rag of an essay that no-one will want to read.

When writers refer to conflict, they don't necessarily mean it in the largest sense of the word. Conflict can, of course, mean warfare, fighting or blazing rows, but in literary terms it includes much smaller ideas. Differences between people in your story can give rise to conflict, without resorting to bloodshed. For instance:

- Your desire to get to university despite a background where you are expected to go out to work at fifteen is an example of conflict
- You wanted to escape the city life and go and live in the country. Your wife didn't. It didn't end in divorce, but it's still conflict
- You fancy a sun-drenched holiday on a Caribbean island, surrounded by hot and cold running waiters; your husband wants to pitch a tent in the Cairngorms. That's conflict.

There is also a type of conflict that we refer to as inner conflict:

- Should I have said what I said?
- What did it take for me to go up in an aeroplane when I was scared stiff of flying?
- Should I have had the last potato when Freda only had three?

Writing conflict is not a technique in itself. When you write conflict, you need to consider some of the other ideas in this section – description, dialogue, flashbacks, atmosphere. Writing conflict is an attitude of mind.

You might argue that conflict is perhaps more the territory of the fiction writer. True, but this section is concerned with how the techniques of the fiction writer can improve your life story writing. You might also argue that there are some superb memoirs of idyllic lives where little seems to go wrong. Again true, but if you examine these stories in detail, you will soon see that all is not as smooth as it might at first look. Things go wrong even in the most perfect of settings:

- The car breaks down on the way to your holiday destination.
- Your mother buys an expensive dress that she then decides she doesn't like, the shop won't take it back and she has to hide all this from your father, who is on an economy drive. The teacher punishes you for flicking an ink pellet, when in fact it was Keith Thomas in the next desk. Immediately this puts you in conflict with both Keith and the teacher.

Even in the calmest seas of life, there are days when it gets a little choppy. Choppy seas are far more interesting than flat ponds. Storm-whipped oceans make for even more interesting reading.

Tension and Pace

The sister skill of using conflict is understanding how to use tension and pace to build up your story.

The simplest way to alter the pace of your story is to alter sentence length. If the action is frantic, we want short, sharp sentences and vocabulary to match. If the sun is shining and you're sipping iced gin and tonic with not a care in the world, then we expect a longer, more measured sentence.

However, don't forget that the length of your paragraphs is at least as important as sentence length. Take a look at any book and you'll see the difference between a long descriptive paragraph and action-filled or dialogue-rich stretches. There's that white space again we encountered in Chapter 8, where we dealt with dialogue.

To keep your general pace up, use good, strong verbs, rather than pairing up a weak verb with an adverb. For instance, if someone 'walked slowly' what exactly are they doing? Could you replace 'walked slowly' with 'ambled', or 'shambled' or 'staggered' or 'limped' or 'sauntered'? Be precise.

Sometimes, writers are simply too wordy. Check for the number of adjectives you have used. We all tend to over-use adjectives and slip in too many. Instead of painting a word-picture, you can quickly bog down your story.

We also over-write. Read your work out loud. Is it easy to read, or do you find yourself stumbling over awkward, over-fancy phrases? If you do, then the reader will as well.

Think about your story in cinematic terms. At the end of a film scene, there are several ways in which we can move onto the next. Sometimes the camera lingers as the hero drives into the distance. Sometimes we cut to something unconnected – a flock of birds flying overhead. Sometimes we leap forward ten years in time with an appropriate sub-title to show us where we are. At other times, there is a slow dissolve as the hypnosis takes effect on the prisoner's mind and we know that we are going to regress to his childhood.

Moving from one scene to the next is an important business. Sometimes, you may be tempted to link two episodes some time apart by writing several paragraphs, perhaps even a chapter. When you read it, you think to yourself, 'This really is boring'. But how else are you going to cover the ground? What's wrong with simply jumping ahead ten years?

Ten years later, I found myself in exactly the same predicament....

It gets your story to where you want it to be and the reader hasn't dozed off during your paragraph (or even chapter) of stodgy filler.

There are other times when you can use a kind of 'jump cut' to great effect. Let's suppose that you are going to write that scene when you and your husband are disagreeing over a holiday destination.

Your husband arrives back from work to find you up to your arm-pits in brochures marked 'Caribbean Paradise' and 'Beat the winter blues and fly somewhere warm'.

Under his arm, he carries three skinny cloth rolls. They turn out to be a two-man bivouac the size of a child's play-tent, which when fully erected gives you headroom of seventeen inches, and two bed mats. He expects to you to put one of these between you and the ground. It's the thickness of a five-pence piece.

You argue for warmth and sunshine. He argues for adventure and hardiness. Your parting shot to him is, 'I'm not going camping in the Cairngorms and that's final'.

Of course, for the sake of our example, you do end up camping in the Cairngorms. If this is a film, what's the best scene to show next?

We could see your husband packing equipment, you both getting into the car, driving to the Cairngorms, pitching the tent, slowly beginning to get colder and colder. Dull. Dull. Dull.

Or, we cut straight to a picture of you shivering in a collapsing tent in sub-zero temperatures, slapping mittened hands round your blanketed body. Sharper. Quicker. Wittier.

Where some people tend to overwrite, others undercook it, so their resulting stories are too skeletal. In an effort to get the facts down, they forget that someone else is going to read their work. If you put the ideas and techniques from this section into practice, thinking about the elements of description, of dialogue, of making the people in your story vibrant characters, then you'll soon find that your writing becomes more fleshed out.

What you write will no longer be the blanched bones of your existence, but something of flesh and blood – a living, breathing story.

The Flashback and Backstory

The Flashback is a really useful device that you will be familiar with from films and books.

It is very easy to start at the beginning, with your birth, and simply carry on writing until you catch up with yourself. There is nothing wrong with this, but if you can shift a little from one time to another, it makes your story all the more interesting. It gives your story a context.

It's a technique that Blake Morrison uses in his book *And When Did You Last See Your Father.* He shifts between timescales, so that we have two stories moving towards a point at which they must converge. The book is about the death of his father, but we open with a chapter describing his father queue-jumping a line of stationary traffic to get to Oulton Park to watch motor-racing. In the next chapter, we are catapulted to the early 1990s (the 'now' of the story if you like) and a visit to his elderly father, recovering from an operation in hospital. Even within this second chapter, we then go back to an earlier event, when his mother has a nasty fall.

A flashback, then, is when you simply slip back in time to a previous episode. But, you then tell it with forward momentum. If you want to make sure that your reader is with you, you can always use a section break to indicate that you've moved to a different time.

Backstory is slightly different. It is more of an insertion of information into an episode, often used to clarify what we're writing about.

We are now aware that each episode of your story needs to start with some kind of action. We've also already seen that if we introduce each new character with a welter of information, it can get rather boring. One way around this is to introduce a character by having them do something – then by filling in something of the character's background later. It's an approach you often see:

'There you go,' said Arthur, lifting an unfeasibly large parcel off his bicycle, 'I'll just check the list with you.'

Arthur pulled out his sheet of paper and began ticking off the items as we put them on the kitchen table.

'One tin of baked beans, catering size... check .... One melon, honeydew ... check ...toilet paper, medicated ... check'

Arthur had been in the RAF. He ran through the routine of delivering groceries as though he were preparing a Lancaster Bomber for a night-time raid. There were some in the village who suggested that the nearest he'd ever been to an aeroplane was Farnborough Air Show, but .....

Backstory works equally well for descriptions of places:

We arrived shortly after midnight. The key was where it always was and we let ourselves in, swiftly lit both fire and stove and began dragging in luggage and groceries from the car.

We'd rented this cottage for the past five years and each year we'd grown to know and love its idiosyncrasies more and more...

In both these examples, cut off mid-flow though they are, we are into the backstory after only a sentence or two. But there is a potential danger with backstory - we don't want too much of it. It stops your story from moving forward and if it is too long will feel clumsy and the reader may even forget where they've got to in the main narrative. Backstory also often comes in the form of information and if you give us too much of that, we're back in infodump territory.

Keep Concrete

Hey, that sounds like an instruction. Or perhaps it's a graffito on a sixties building about to be pulled down. 'Keep concrete!' Let me explain:

When we write, it is very easy to end up using abstract vocabulary that doesn't actually show the reader a great deal. We describe someone as 'beautiful', we write things like 'it was very evocative', 'Paris is lovely', 'the view was indescribable' (that one should be a criminal offence).

Some people would condemn this as lazy writing. It isn't. It's natural writing. It's when we come to revise our work and don't change it for something better that we're being lazy. Even the greatest of writers are capable of scattering their first drafts with these abstract terms.

If you look through your work and find something like 'Granddad was eccentric', mark it up with a highlighter pen. The reason why you need to spot items like this is that you're not being specific. What the reader wants to know is how was he eccentric? Did he bathe in asses' milk? Did he wear geraniums on his head on the Sabbath? Did children run screaming from him when they caught sight of him?

'The hills were gorgeous at that time of year.' What was gorgeous about them? Were the leaves on the trees changing colour? Was it the effect of sunlight on snow? Was it the dry stone walls and the sheep? What was it that made you stop and look at those hills and say, 'these hills are gorgeous'?

'Keep Concrete' is the first cousin of 'show, don't tell', which we examined in more detail back in Chapter 5. Yes, another card to tape to your monitor!

Writing Lists

Sometimes, you will find that you need to write a list. Perhaps they're the items you kept in you school desk, or maybe it's all the kit the army expected you to carry when you went on a training march, or the contents of your mother's handbag. You need to think of ways in which to make this interesting. A list helps to get through a lot of material in a short time.

Here's the great Harpo Marx (remember him - curly blond hair, mute, harp?) on the relevance of his school education to a poor child in the big city:

Another complaint that I had was that school taught you about holidays you could never afford to celebrate, like Thanksgiving and Christmas. It didn't teach you about real holidays like St Patrick's Day when you could watch a parade for free, or Election Day, when you could make a giant bonfire in the middle of the street and the cops wouldn't stop you. School didn't teach you what to do when you were stopped by an enemy gang - when to run, when to stand your ground. School didn't teach you how to collect tennis balls, build a scooter, ride the El trains and trolleys, hitch onto delivery wagons, own a dog, go for a swim, get a chunk of ice or a piece of fruit - all without paying a cent.

School didn't teach you which hockshops would give you dough without asking where you got your merchandise, or how to

shoot pool or bet on a poker hand or where to sell junk or how to find sleeping room in a bed with four other brothers.
Harpo Speaks by Harpo Marx,
First published in 1961

You can also use a list to good effect if you want to bring out some aspect of a place or a person. In the following extract, Mrs Winterson walks her adoptive daughter, Jeanette, through the local high street and we get a picture of both the town and Mrs Winterson:

We went past Woolworths – 'A Den of Vice'. Past Marks and Spencer's – 'The Jews killed Christ'. Past the funeral parlour and the pie shop – 'They share an oven'. Past the biscuit stall and its moon-faced owners – 'Incest'. Past the pet parlour – 'Bestiality'. Past the bank – 'Usury'. Past the Citizens Advice Bureau – 'Communists'. Past the day nursery – 'Unmarried mothers'. Past the pawnbroker's where my mother had once tried to pawn her leftover solid gold tooth, and on at last to a caff called the Palatine for beans on toast.
Why Be Happy When You Could Be Normal? by Jeanette Winterson,
First published in 2011

Notice, of course, that this list does more than just give us bald information. As well as getting a snapshot of the types of shops and other establishments, Mrs Winterson's running commentary provides us with a humorous insight into her character. We know so much about her just from this one short extract. It's a fantastic use of a list and, importantly, doesn't carry on for too long.

If you're going to write a list, then you need to keep it both reasonably short and try to add extra details to it that will make it interesting for the reader.

Using Humour

If you can add humour to your work, it can improve it immeasurably. The difficulty is that it is highly individual. What makes one person roll on the floor with laughter makes another person cringe. You may not be trying to make your life story a hysterical, laugh-out-loud read, but leavening it with little anecdotes, well-chosen phrases, and vignettes of larger-than-life people will add interest for the reader.

Here's Jeanette Winterson again. She refers to her adoptive mother, a religious fundamentalist, as 'Mrs Winterson'. In this truncated extract, Winterson manages to portray her as a comic figure whilst all the time her behaviour is appalling. I suspect that humour is used here as a means of dealing with an upbringing by someone as irrational as Mrs Winterson, from whose mouth comes the question that her daughter uses for this autobiography.

Mrs. Winterson was not a welcoming woman. If anyone knocked at the door she ran down the lobby and shoved the poker through the letter-box.

I reminded her that angels often came in disguise and she said that was true but they didn't come disguised in Crimplene. ...

... The only time that Mrs Winterson liked to answer the door was when she knew that the Mormons were coming round.

Then she waited in the lobby, and before they had dropped the knocker she had flung open the door waving her Bible and warning them of eternal damnation. This was confusing for the Mormons because they thought they were in charge of eternal damnation. But Mrs Winterson was a better candidate for the job.

Why Be Happy When You Could Be Normal? by Jeanette Winterson,
First published in 2011

When done with thought and attention to detail, a short, pithy list can work extremely well.

Over to You
Making a List

Think about the lists written by Harpo Marx and Jeannette Winterson. Where might you make a list in your life story? It might be something such as:

- Your mother's funeral instructions
- Things you have left behind in the pub
- The cars you've owned
- Pets you've kept
- Food you refuse to eat
- Shrubs you've planted
- Sweets you ate as a child
- Records you bought as a teenager
- Boys/girls you fancied at school

Choose something where you think a list would work and try writing it, making sure that you add a little description for each item. For example:

My first car was a Ford Cortina. It died of rust, as did my Fiat 128 and my Renault 4, which was reliable, but noisy and required me to take paracetamol before any long journey. I followed this up with another Fiat, then fed up with smaller cars, traded that in for a Talbot which was as deeply unfashionable as any of the other cars I'd had...

****

Section 3

Editing and Polishing

Whatever sentence will bear to be read twice, we may be sure was thought twice. Henry David Thoreau

Well done on getting this far.

Assuming you've put everything we've looked at into practice, you've now written your life story in scintillating prose that has atmosphere, tension, pace, coruscating dialogue and an opening that will pin your reader to the floor.

If you think you've finished, I've got some bad news for you. You're about to start rewriting it all. It's a tough old world, so pour yourself a cup of tea or something stronger before we move on to the next stage.

Chapter 11

Rewriting, Revising and Editing Your Work

In the last section, we looked at the creative side of writing. I hope that I've given you the confidence to write as well as you can.

If you cast your mind even further back, in Chapter 4, I wrote about encouraging Writing Brain to take over whilst you are in writing mode. This is a great way of filling the page (or the computer screen) as quickly as is humanly possible. However, unless you are an absolute genius it is unlikely that you can spill out several hundred words without having to revise them in some way.

Yes, there are days when we write freely and our words flow easily. Sometimes, we need to make only the slightest of changes to what we've written. But we do need to make changes. On other days, the words that dribble out will form a lumpy porridge that needs complete revision, or possibly even eradication.

Looking over what you have written, and then re-writing where you think it is necessary, is what separates the poor amateur from the accomplished writer. It really is as straightforward as that. As the playwright Sheridan once wrote 'easy writing's cursed hard reading'. Sentences that flow smoothly when you read the final version may have started out as clumsy, awkward clumps of words. The professional writer takes these infelicities and moulds and shapes them into something smooth and easy to read.

We're about to do the same thing with your manuscript. Now that we've accomplished our task of getting our story down on paper comes the hard part of re-working it to make it the best we can. We've got to bring that Editing Brian, the critical, analytical part, to the forefront. You need this little chap if you are going to sharpen up what you've written and make your reader want to read on.

Don't think that the process of rewriting, revising and editing your work needs to be a dull slog. For some people, re-writing is much more enjoyable than the writing itself. Some writers prefer the languid pace of honing, polishing and re-shaping to the hard graft of actually getting words down onto that blank piece of paper.

However, if you are new to writing, you might find this the hardest part. Suddenly, instead of adding words to the page, you're subtracting them. You find yourself crossing out whole paragraphs that took ages to write. Everything you have written goes under the microscope and you have to become your own stern critic. Sometimes it feels a little like you have been building your own house for months on end and you have to demolish the whole of a gable end to put something right.

Types of Revision

One of the problems we have when we talk about revising or editing your work is that this can mean anything from removing an entire chapter (or even more), to inserting or deleting a comma. Some authors of how-to-write books suggest a fixed number of times that you revise a work. Some also suggest that you wait until you have finished all your writing before you start revising.

As you can tell, I'm not a great one for trying to lay down golden rules as to how something should or should not be done. Besides, you will by now have developed a whole range of strategies for getting your writing done; you will in turn also develop your own methods and approaches for revising your work.

As revision/editing can mean so many different things, let's look at what that implies for you as an author.

Big Revision

At the mega-level, to get the widest possible view, before you start getting down to the nitty-gritty, I think it is worth reading your finished manuscript all the way through. However, if you do this the minute you've typed the last full stop on the last page, you may find that you are too close to what you have written to be objective in your opinions. Many writers like to put a manuscript away in a desk drawer for a few weeks, even months, before coming back to it. This gives them a chance to read the work almost as though it were written by someone else. But let's be realistic. Leaving your freshly-printed manuscript to one side for three months is a tough demand. You'll probably be hankering to fiddle with it as soon as you can, tarting it up ready for someone else to read it.

If you can leave it to lie fallow for a few weeks, you will find that it will do you a power of good. It will give both mind and body time to recuperate from the hard slog and your words will seem so much fresher to you, almost as if someone else wrote them.

On the other hand, there are many writers who start each day's writing session by re-reading what they wrote the previous day, making revisions and alterations where they see fit and using this almost like a warm-up exercise for the writing session ahead.

151

There are a couple of problems with this kind of revision.

First, you are revising at a micro-level. Imagine that yesterday you wrote an episode of 1,500 words about the time you were caught stealing chewing-gum from the corner shop (shame on you!). You will be able to alter all sorts of things in the piece – grammar, spelling, punctuation, cheesy phrases, bits where you've tried too hard to sound like a real writer. What you won't be able to sense is if that episode fits into the overall pattern of your book.

Second, you can get caught up in the process of revision and spend hours fiddling with a sentence, writing it one way then another, whereas what you really need to be doing is getting more words down onto paper.

A sensible compromise might be to start each day with a little light re-writing, just to get warmed up, but not to get caught-up in-depth. Don't worry if you end up cutting a whole episode or even a chapter or more. It may seem entirely painful at first. In fact, it may be painful to you no matter how often you do it, but even if you never get used to it, you will eventually become resigned to the fact that it has to be done.

Stick with the Big Picture

When you do come to read the first draft of your manuscript, it is tempting to take a red pen to it and flag up every little spelling mistake and clumsy phrase. In fact, it's almost impossible not to do this. Sometimes you'll wonder if you ever learnt any English at all, when you come across sentences or paragraphs that mean absolutely nothing. It's difficult, but at this stage you should try to avoid getting too deeply into the minutiae of your manuscript. You need to be reading it from an almost structural point-of-view.

For instance, imagine you have written a 100,000 words manuscript – I know I said we were aiming for around half that, but you've worked extremely hard. When you come to read it, you realise that although the book is supposed to be about your whole life, three-quarters of it is in fact about your childhood in India at the end of the Second World War.

You may decide that this makes your book rather unbalanced. You have used 75,000 words to describe ten years of your life and 25,000 words to tell us about the other sixty. Hard though it is, you probably need to lose as much as a quarter of the book if you are to concentrate purely on that Indian childhood.

Don't throw yourself off the nearest cliff if this happens to you. If you simply remove the 25,000 words about your later life, you can keep them in another file on your computer and use it as the start of Volume Two.

At this stage in your revision process, you should be asking yourself such questions as:

- Does the book feel balanced?
- Which sections work particularly well?
- Which sections don't work well? Should they be improved, or removed? Are they too thin or too fat?
- Is there anything I have left out that would improve the overall structure of the book?

At this stage, you should also be loath to pass on your manuscript for anyone else to read. Most people are used to reading finished, polished works. They probably don't understand what a book reads like in the early stages of its development.

It's also extremely difficult to know whose opinion is best. If you ask someone whose main literary diet is breathless thrillers to read your gentle story of an idyllic rural childhood – the kind of book they would never read even if given it for Christmas – then you are not going to get a balanced reply. Your book is simply not their kind of book – no matter how well (or badly) written it might be.

You even have to be careful of asking your spouse or partner to read it. They are notoriously incapable of giving any rational opinion. Either they will love it simply because it is you who have written it or, and I'm afraid this is all too common, they will simply pick out a few spelling mistakes and some mangled sentences and all your hard work is damned in two minutes of nit-picking.

I can't stress strongly enough that this is probably not a good stage at which to ask someone to read your work. It is still too personal and you still have a lot of revision to do. After all that hard work, it is so easy for you to be knocked back by an unkind word. You might prefer instead to move to the next stage of revision

Revising for Energy

We all want our work to have 'energy'. We want the words to come alive; we want them to rise up off the page. At some point in the revision process, you need to be looking at what you've written to see if it will engage your reader. If it lies flat on the page, it won't.

Writing too much is one of the modern curses. Owning a computer makes it extremely easy to hack words into a machine. But don't worry if you have written too much. In fact, on the contrary, you should be ecstatic, because it gives you far more material to work with. Indeed, cutting things is harder if you've only got a few words down in the first place.

Imagine you've sat down to write for a couple of hours and have written 1,000 words. Later, you're reading over what you've written and you suddenly realise that 800 of them are listless, lifeless and pointless. If you cut all those words, suddenly that writing session becomes a stingy 200 words. It may hurt to get rid of 80% of what you've written, but ask yourself a question. Do you want to be the author of 1,000 mediocre words, or to have written a great piece of 200 words?

Ideally, you'd have liked to have produced a cracking piece of a thousand words straight off. Wouldn't we all? Unfortunately, the writing life isn't like that. Hard though it is, your best course of action is to get out your coloured pen and excise the dull bits. So, whenever you read over a piece you have written, you need to ask yourself the questions:

- Is it interesting?
- Will this make the reader read on?
- Is it exciting/engaging/endearing?
- Does it touch on human emotions?
- Have I tried to be a bit too clever-clever?
- Am I telling when I should be showing?
- Have I got action and dialogue?
- Am I writing in scenes?

If you feel that what you've written doesn't do these things, then you need to be prepared to alter or even cut what you've written.

There may be occasions on which what you have written feels too skeletal. You want some flesh on the bones. For instance, you might have introduced a character who you thought would play a minor role in your recounting of your life story. On re-reading, you find that this character is more important to your story than you had expected. Perhaps the reader needs to know more about this character, more about his/her background. Here is a bona fide case for adding material.

There's nothing wrong with this. Revision isn't simply a process of subtraction. However, be warned. Sometimes, when you introduce new material, it can alter the overall structure of what you are writing. Also, it is very easy to end up padding out your work to fill space. This, of course, flies in the face of what you are trying to do, which is to make what you've written crisp, energetic, and reader-friendly.

Editing for Meaning

If you have been through the processes outlined above, you have done the hardest work of all. Everything from now on in is just a process of 'tarting up' your manuscript. It still requires you to have your wits about you, but the big decisions have now been made. It is very important now to check through your work to make sure that what you have written says what you want it to say.

One of the first things to check is the words you have used. It is very easy to become 'writerly' and start using long words. These don't normally impress readers; they put them off. So, it is important to ensure that anyone reading your book can understand what it is you are trying to tell them.

If, for instance, you are hoping to sell your book *Thirty Years in the Nuclear Industry* to the general public, then you need to make sure that the book is written at a level that the general public will understand. A book filled with the jargon of nuclear science will probably only appeal to a handful of physicists. It may not even appeal to your family.

One of the most frequent mistakes made by new writers is that their sentences are too long. Now, this doesn't mean that you have to insult the reader by making every sentence comprise six words. However, you need to bear in mind that long, complex writing with too little punctuation will put off the vast majority of readers. Even people with the most highly-developed reading habits will blanch at wading through sentences that spill out for fifty-plus words. Be careful of wordiness.

Editing for Spelling, Grammar and Punctuation

As soon as you mention spelling, grammar or punctuation, out come the hawks. Whenever I teach this aspect of writing, somehow my classes dissolve into debates on the state of education in schools.

The pendulum swings in every walk of life. In children's education we have gone from an educational system where accuracy was far more important than originality, through days when 'creativity' and 'free thought' were more important than clarity, to the modern system where children of 6 are forced to explain the difference between a gerund and a gerundive even before they're capable of tying their own shoe-laces.

Often with my classes, I meet the two extreme results of the British system. I have students who are terrified of setting a word on paper for fear of putting a comma in the wrong place. They find themselves sitting alongside students who will produce, at the drop of a hat, reams of material that defies all known grammar systems.

Let me state clearly that I think that spelling, grammar and punctuation are extremely important. I hate it when I misspell anything and when I come across one of my sentences in which I have mangled the English language beyond tolerable belief, I cringe. I can't make up my mind whether the apostrophe should be banned, or if I should equip myself with a fat red pen and run riot amongst the market stalls of Britain.

Knowing the actual vocabulary of grammar is useful in a limited way. It's handy to know what nouns, verbs, adjectives and a handful of other terms mean. Most of the rest is technical and is largely specialist jargon.

Whilst spelling is not a matter of personal choice – most words have one or perhaps two spellings - punctuation and grammar are more slippery eels. The concept of 'correct' English is extremely hard to pin down. Language is constantly changing and evolving. There are aspects of those changes that can be very annoying. I find 'prevaricate', which means to tell a lie, used instead of procrastinate particularly irritating. I also get wound-up by 'aggravating' for 'irritating', 'momentarily', when used for 'in a moment' and 'infer' misused for 'imply'. 'Amount' for 'number' and 'less' for 'fewer' also get to me, but I really should relax.

Those are some of my bug-bears; I'm sure you have some of your own. However, try not to get too hot under the collar about 'correct' usage, but strive to be clear and precise in what you write. Whilst I can swing from pedant to profligate in the same sentence, I still believe you can get too hung up on these issues whilst you are actually in the process of writing your book. It can stop you from making progress. If you are too worried that your English is 'correct', then it can mean that the end result of your work, even after much revising, is stilted and stuffy.

If you have tried to write in such a way as to make your story conversational, it is sometimes hard to apply the strictest of grammar rules. Normally, for instance, a sentence needs a verb (a doing word) to be a sentence. However, you can write sentences without verbs. Like this one. Dickens did. And me. Why not you?

But it should be stressed that you still can't ignore all the reasonable demands of grammar if your readers are to make head or tail of your work. So, if you find grammar and/or punctuation difficult, get down to your local bookshop and buy yourself a book on the subject. At the risk of inserting an advert, you could always try my book *Writing Good, Plain English*.

If you find that your sentences are longer than they need to be, one useful trick to shorten them is to replace some of the commas you have used with a full-stop. This won't work every time, but will help. Similarly, check for 'ands' and 'buts'. There's nothing wrong in using these, but you may find that you have linked two very long clauses that would read better if separated by a full stop.

Proofreading

The kind of editing where you are looking for spelling, grammar and punctuation mistakes is often referred to as proofreading. It is the very last stage of any editing process. Some people might see it as nit-picking. I think this is a mistake. Publishers allow for the fact that their authors are human (I typed that as 'there authors' incidentally and didn't spot it straight away). They don't mind the occasional mistake. However, a manuscript that is full of misspellings, bad punctuation and mangled grammar is not going to improve your chances of finding favour with your readers, let alone any publishing success.

Don't rely on your computer's spellchecker, either. Spellcheckers are extremely useful tools for spotting when you have written 'usfeul' instead of 'useful'. However, if like me, your fingers are awkward, lumpen and don't ever seem to hit the keys in the order in which your brain is sending out signals, then you will end up with plenty of words that are misspelled, but that are perfectly valid words in their own right. For instance, I am forever typing 'form' instead of 'from' and vice versa. We all know the difference between 'two', 'to' and 'too', but it is very easy to type in the wrong one whilst your brain is racing. Typos are inevitable. In addition, no matter how good your spelling, punctuation and so forth, it is extraordinarily difficult to pick up your own mistakes. Your eye will tend to see what it expects to see; this can lead to its playing tricks on you. It is at this stage in the editing process that you could call on someone else to take a look at your manuscript. You need someone who has a good standard of English, but not someone who is too pedantic. I got picked up on my spelling of the word *fogy* and was told that I had misspelled it. It should be *fogey*. The same has happened to me with the word *carcases* or *carcasses*. *Fogy* and *fogey* and *carcases* and *carcasses* are correct. Provided you bribe your proofreading friend with enough drink, they should check things like that out for you.

So, to sum up, don't confuse re-writing your work with tidying up the spelling and grammar. They are separate issues. Try not to slip into proofreader mode when looking at the bigger picture.

Chapter 12

Pitfalls for the Life Story Writer

In the last chapter, I tried to concentrate on positive ways of making your writing as good as you can. Here, I'm going to look at some of the traps you can fall into and how to put them right.

Carmen Miranda Syndrome

For those of you too young to remember, Carmen Miranda was a South American singer who could wear an entire fruit bowl on her head whilst simultaneously warbling out songs. Honestly. Her most famous song was *I-I-I-I like you very much* in which every time she came to the word *I*, she repeated it a handful of times.

As you're writing about yourself, you may find that you end up using the word *I* a lot. In fact, it's inevitable. The trouble is with *I* is that it can exaggerate the effect of everything in your book. So, when you are quite reasonably having a minor crow about a success, it can turn you into a vainglorious, boasting egotist. Similarly, if you are describing troubled times, it can make you sound like a whingeing, whining defeatist. There are some straightforward ways to reduce the I-I-I effect.

The most useful technique is to avoid starting sentences and especially paragraphs with the word *I*. Somehow, having the word at the start of a sentence, and more importantly at the start of a paragraph, makes it stand out.

I went inside because the door was already open.

… can easily be re-written as…

As the door was already open, I went inside.

Placing the *I* mid-sentence stops it being as intrusive.

Check openings to sentences and especially paragraphs to see if you have used *I* too much. You can always mark them up with a highlighter pen on your draft if it helps. If you have too many, think of ways to change the word order to take the emphasis away from it or re-write the sentence completely.

If your story can take it, why not talk to the reader from time to time? Perhaps use this chat with the reader as a way of moving into a new phase of the story. For instance, if you're writing about how your memory fails you from time to time, you could write something like this:

We've all had them. You know what I'm talking about. The fridge moments. We're looking for the boot polish, the radio, the cat and we're standing, staring at the inside of the fridge wondering how on earth we ever got there.

Well, things have moved beyond the fridge moment.

I don't know if this has ever happened to you. You're walking down the street and you see someone. You know that person. You know them well. You've known them for years. You know where they live, how many children they have, what their husband has for lunch on Thursdays. You know everything it's

*decently possible to know about them, except for the life of you,
you can't remember their name.*

That's exactly what happened to me in July of that year.

As well as avoiding the over-use of the first-person pronoun,
this technique also draws the reader into the story. Shared
experience helps to overcome the 'egotism' of a life story.

Shifting the camera onto different people in your story also
means that you stop using *I* too much.

Reginald Bowler came into my life on the 13th March 1953.
'Working for me, son, is like being part of a marriage.'

*He forgot to add that it was a marriage made in hell. Each
day, as I totted up the columns of pounds, shillings and pence, Reg
sat behind a mound of papers, alternately sucking his tea and his
teeth. Occasionally, he would unwind a paperclip and chase stray
bits of meat around what remained of his molars.*

By placing the camera on Reg, we have now moved our
focus onto a description of him. We can write about Reg now and
the emphasis is no longer on us. The occasional stray *I* will hardly
be noticeable as we will be concentrating on the appalling Reginald
Bowler.

Telling Us Too Much About Yourself

One of the major decisions you need to make when writing any
kind of autobiography is how much you want to reveal to the
reader. I know this may seem an odd thing to say – after all, you're
writing an autobiography. But at one extreme of autobiographical

writing is the hugely confessional writing that tells us everything about you and your family and everyone you've ever met.

This kind of writing has a function. It is often referred to as 'writing out the demons'. Sometimes things happen in our lives that are so awful that we look for ways in which we can come to terms with them. Writing about these events is one way of doing this. It's great therapy.

I'm not convinced that what you write when you do this should be for anything more than your personal consumption, however. Whilst it might do you a power of good to get the matter off your chest, it doesn't always do the same for the reader. What was catharsis to you may well look like self-indulgence to others.

Imagine your book as a guest at a dinner party. That guest spends all dinner party twining on about how hard their life has been and how unfair it all is. Whilst you might be able to lend a sympathetic ear for a few minutes, after a while, you feel like you've been made to sit next to a rain cloud. Everyone else round the table seems to be having witty, animated sunny conversations, but you've been lumped next to someone who's been paid by the Samaritans to drum up custom.

You may not have meant what you write to sound like a whinge, but when you read it back, it sounds like one long rant. Frankly, who wants to know? If your whole tone is depressive and self-pitying, then nobody in their right mind is going to get further than a couple of pages before giving up.

'Aha,' you reply, 'but my life has been hard. I've had a lot of bad breaks.'

Believe me, I'm not for one moment trying to belittle anyone who has had a tough time. If you've been unlucky, write about it with wit and passion. Or else, write about it in a whingeing and moaning fashion, then burn your manuscript. You've got it off your chest now. Hopefully, you might feel a little better for having written out those demons.

Even at a more restrained level, you will have to make some decisions as to what to leave in and what to take out of your work. If you include the incident when Aunty Doris got drunk at Aunty Flo's funeral and sang the Marseillaise whilst wearing a tea-cosy, what repercussions might this have? Will Aunty Doris's children take umbrage? Will others think it sacrilegious to the memory of Saintly Aunty Flo?

You'd be surprised how many toes you could tread on in even the most straightforward of tales, without breaking the law of libel (I will deal with libel later in this chapter). However, do be warned that some members of your family might see Aunty Doris's behaviour as belonging to that bank of family secrets that shouldn't be paraded in public.

Similarly, you might well think that the most interesting people you can write about are your family's black sheep – and yes, you're right, they're far more interesting than the law-abiding, morally incorruptible ones with steady jobs. Others might see any re-telling of tales about these black sheep as bringing shame on the family.

If in doubt, get someone whose opinion you trust to cast an eye over any sections of your writing that you think might cause upset. You might find that just by toning down one or two aspects of the story, you can tell it without offence yet still make it a good read.

Regional and Specialist Matters

We've already dealt with regional dialect and accent in Chapter 8. All regions also have their own vocabularies. An alley in one part of the country becomes a lonning in another and a ginnel in yet another.

Similarly, all trades and professions have their own vocabularies. For anyone who does not know either an area of the country or the language of a particular trade, using jargon or dialect words can be off-putting if they are not used with care.

There are three main ways of dealing with this. The first is to give a direct explanation:

Arthur had brought his bait box with him. A bait box (unsurprisingly enough) contained your 'bait', in other words your mid-morning snack or lunch.

The second is to make it obvious from the context:

Every time we shuffled into the ginnel I felt nervous. It was dark and damp along there, and there was hardly room even for a six-year old to stretch out his arms. If you did, you could feel the walls of the back yards on either side of you, walls that rose up tall above your head, making the space seem even more enclosed.

The third is quite simply to provide a glossary of terms:

Bait box: a box in which you put sandwiches for your mid-morning snack.

Writing Economically – Sticking to the Point

A frequent beginner's mistake is to give us far more detail than we really want to know. We've all come across this sort of story:

> *I was sipping my cup of tea and watching the ten o'clock news, when suddenly there was a ring at the door.*
>
> *'Who could that be at ten o'clock in the evening?' I asked myself.*
>
> *I got up from the armchair, crossed the room and went down the hall to the front door, which I had carefully locked at around 7.30 that very evening.*
>
> *'Hi, Carole.' It was David. 'I hope it's not too late. I know it's ten o'clock, but I saw the lights were on.'*

Not only is this tooth-gnashingly dismal, but how is the reader to know what information is important? Is it the fact that it's ten o'clock at night? After all, the writer has managed to mention the fact three times in the space of a handful of sentences.

Who knows? But let's assume that the following information is relevant:

- Carole is relaxing
- It's 10 o'clock at night
- David is apologetic about calling round so late

What's wrong with:

> *One evening, I was relaxing in front of the 10 o'clock news, when the doorbell rang. A hugely apologetic David greeted me.*

The second piece is less than one third the length of the first. It is easier to read, far less boring and contains all the same information. This is when writing narrative summary comes in handy.

(See Chapter 5 if you need a refresher on the topic of narrative summary.)

Sounding Dated or Wordy

When we are learning to use language – at school, college, and university – we are encouraged to develop our vocabulary and grammar. Quite right too. If we didn't, we'd all be ignoramuses (or should that be ignorami?). As a result, we are often left with the impression that the longer a word and the more complex the sentence, the better.

If we are to be writers, and more importantly writers who are read, what we must learn is a sense of self-discipline. Education is there to develop us. I'm quite proud that I know the meanings of words like 'meretricious' and 'chthonic', but until just now I've never found a place to use them.

There's nothing wrong with good grammar (or long words). It helps to know the rules in order to break them and a wide vocabulary gives you plenty of tools as a writer. However, if you write your life story in the same style as you would have used for a school history essay, then it will be dull fare. And your first duty to your reader is to entertain. *Make 'em laugh, make 'em cry*, as the saying goes. Of course you want to inform the reader about your life, but don't push that information to the front so that what you've written is a laundry list.

Language also has a nasty habit of dating very quickly. Victorian novelists had page upon page in which they could churn out complex sentences. The leisured classes who read their books had fewer distractions than the modern reader. Even books written only fifty years ago often seem very old-fashioned, staid and long-winded.

It's important to make your words resonate down the generations. If your life story already sounds as though it was written a hundred years ago, how dated will it sound in another fifty years?

To avoid this, try making your writing sound as though you are talking to the reader, then you will find that you end up with a readable style. It may not be the style that would have your English teacher whooping it up in the classroom, but you're not writing for her any more.

Telling the Truth

Unless you're using your life as a freewheeling basis for a novel, then, you must make the effort to be as honest as you possibly can in your writing.

Of course, truth is subjective. It's an individual matter. Ask three neutral eyes witnesses to give accounts of the same incident and you will end up with three different versions. You can, at best, give only your version of the truth. But your version is rather different than pure invention. Start inventing facts and episodes, people and places and you're beginning to breech the contract that you have with your reader, who is almost certainly assuming that you are playing fair.

Indeed, there are well-publicized cases of life writers who've invented too many elements of their stories and faced a backlash as a result. Perhaps the most famous of these is the case of James Frey and his memoir of drug addiction *A Million Little Pieces*. Frey over-dramatized his problems. He even included elements that were entirely invented to make himself appear like a hardened ghetto criminal rather than a middle-class kid who'd just got too heavily into drugs.

On the other hand, if you are writing a work that is simply based on matters autobiographical and not pretending it's really your life story, then you can allow yourself a far greater degree of flexibility as regards 'the truth'. You still need to tread very carefully. If your aunt, who is really the world's most generous soul, is portrayed as a stingy miser who allowed her daughter to sleep outside in a snowdrift, then you are straying into very dangerous territory indeed. You are now entering the world of libel.

Libel

Libel is a complicated subject, one that is well beyond the bounds of this book, but which is something that needs to be borne in mind nonetheless.

Essentially, you commit a libel if you make a defamatory statement about an identifiable living person, or a company that is still trading. 'Identifiable' seems to be the key word, so even by disguising 'Sowerby Brothers Meat Products' as 'Southern Sisters Pork Pies', you may not be avoiding potential libel. Similarly, if you defame the character of your headteacher without once mentioning her name, but we can infer who that person is, you could also be committing a libel.

There are several defences to an accusation of libel. First, you can plead 'justification'. In other words, that everything you wrote about that person was true. You probably need potential witnesses to back you up. Just because it has been widely reported by the press that Euphonius P. Buckwheat is a sexual pervert is no defence either. If, in fact, there is no evidence that poor old Mr. Buckwheat is a pervert, then you have committed a libel just as much as the source from which you repeated it.

Second, you can argue that what you have said is 'fair comment'. You are allowed to have opinions about people. However, you will also have to show that you acted without malice.

Your third line of defence is that of 'privilege'. This defence is normally used by newspapers and magazines when they publish something about, for instance, a member of parliament that they deem to be in the public interest.

The fourth and last line of defence probably won't apply to you. It is called 'innocent dissemination' and is mainly applicable to broadcasting or Internet companies who may have disseminated a libel, but without having anything to do with its creation.

You can't libel the dead. However, if an inference can be made by descendants that what is said for the dead could also be applied to them, then you may have committed a libel. If you write:

It's hardly surprising that Edmond Snodgrass was a thief. His father had been a thief and his father before him, like all of Edmond Snodgrass's other relatives.

Despite the fact that Edmond, Edmond's father and Edmond's grandfather are all dead, as are all the relatives to whom you meant to refer, Edmond Snodgrass's nephew is still alive and kicking. You've clearly stated that all the relatives are thieves, thus impugning the surviving nephew. Now, the nephew might take exception to this and bring about a libel action.

'Oh, sorry, I meant the others and not you,' is unlikely to be any form of defence.

There are sharks in the waters of libel. A libel case is often long, extremely expensive and even the winners don't seem to win. The only person to come out smiling in a libel case is a lawyer. The best way to avoid a suit for libel, is not to libel anyone in the first place.

Copyright

If you print anything that you have not written yourself, you may be in breach of copyright.

Deliberately copying someone else's work verbatim is known as plagiarism and is frowned on in the extreme. If you publish anything that looks as though you have simply transferred paragraphs into your own manuscript and are passing it off as your own work, you could be heading for serious trouble. You can be sued for plagiarism, have your work forcibly withdrawn from sale – possibly pulped – and you could be in for some heavy financial losses.

Quoting from other works is, however, acceptable, providing you do so within strict limits. Limit yourself to 300-400 words from a single full-length book and a line or two of poetry and you shouldn't go too far wrong. If you want to use any more than this, then you must obtain the copyright owner's permission for which you will probably also be expected to pay a fee. The cost for song lyrics is enormous. At the time of writing, and specifically in the United Kingdom, this rule normally doesn't apply if an author has been dead for more than seventy years as their work should no longer be in copyright.

It's also worth remembering a couple of other useful things:

You might want to reproduce photographs in your memoir. The person who took the photograph is normally the copyright holder, although this can vary. For instance, if the photograph was taken by an employee as part of his/her work for a company, then copyright probably rests with the company.

Copyright for letters remains with the person who wrote the letter, not the recipient. So, if you want to include a letter that was written to you, you need the copyright owner's permission.

As a rule of thumb, if in doubt, either seek permission or ask yourself if you really need this particular item. You might be surprised at how much easier it is to go without something than it is to track down the copyright owner and then ask permission.

****

Chapter 13

Preparing Your Manuscript

Practical Issues for the Writer

If you have handwritten your work, it may be fine to keep as a memento, but if you want to do anything more with it, then you will definitely need a typed version. If you have the typing skills and some knowledge of computers, obviously you can do this yourself.

Typing up your own work from a handwritten draft can be a very useful process. Some writers I know do this themselves. Somehow, they feel comfortable writing with pen and paper– it's what they were brought up on. Then, when they transfer their hand-written story to the computer, they can make changes as they do so. This means that the first draft becomes a second draft even as they are typing it up. What appears on their computer screens has already had some revising, editing and polishing.

Being brought up on pen and paper, I normally jot down notes by hand and use a notebook because that keeps everything together and different notebooks can suit different purposes. Some folks now take notes on mobile phones, or even dictate the odd snippet that way. But when it comes to the actual process of writing, working directly onto a computer most of the time seems the simplest way of doing it.

There are huge advantages in having your work on a computer. If you type your manuscript on a typewriter and then decide to add a couple of paragraphs, it probably means retyping the whole manuscript. With a computer, if you want to do this, you can easily insert text. If you want to move some information from page eight to page eighty, you can do so with a handful of keyboard strokes or a flash of the mouse. You don't have to buy expensive software either. There are plenty of apps that can be legally downloaded free-of-charge that do just about anything the most expensive brand will do.

If you can't type and have never used a computer, local libraries (if you still have one) are excellent. Besides, buying computer kit is cheaper now than it ever has been, so you can pick up a bargain almost everywhere you look.

You can also use dictation software. This allows you to talk directly into a microphone and the computer cleverly changes your spoken word into the written word. If you use this technique, then you may find it easiest to handwrite your stories first, then read them into the computer, otherwise you may find that your life story largely consists of 'ums' and 'ers'. You may also find that you have to spend some time training the software to recognize your voice.

However, if you don't want to do your own typing and have an aversion to machines, there are people who will be able to do it for you. Putting a wanted advert in your local paper, parish news or shop window or getting a friend to post something on a local website, should bring you to someone who can do the job for you. Typing services are not as thick on the ground as they once were - presumably because more and more people do their own typing. However, if you do find someone to do the job for you make sure you get a copy saved into some kind of digital format - perhaps on a memory stick - as well as on paper. If the paper copy goes missing or is damaged, then you can always have another copy printed from the disk.

Always make sure you have copies of what you've written. If you do your work on the computer, always make a back-up onto disk, a memory stick, an external hard drive or one of the cloud-based storage systems that have appeared over the last few years. Most cloud storage providers offer a minimal amount of storage for free. Here speaks the voice of bitter experience. I once lost an entire chapter of a book - an entire week's work. I still don't think that my 'new' version was as good as the first.

If you are thinking about publishing your life story – in any form – then access to technology is vital. So, let's assume that you now have your work on a computer, what are you going to do with it?

Selling Excerpts from Your Life Story as Articles

As the average age of the population increases, so too does the boom in magazines aimed at the older market. This has meant a growth in the market for nostalgia articles.

Now, don't think that this means that nostalgia articles are easy to sell. As with all sectors of the market, editors are flooded with work. And, the more people buy computers and digital cameras, the more they bombard magazines with material. Some of it is highly usable; a great deal is terrible dross. A while ago, I was talking to the editor of a well-known regional magazine. He told me that he was inundated with twee pieces telling all about the author's schooldays in the area. It wasn't that he would never publish a piece on someone's schooldays, it's just that the piece would either have to be by someone well-known or would have to be so wonderful that he couldn't resist it.

Look round the shelves of your local magazine shop. Titles such as *Evergreen, This England, The Oldie,* and *The People's Friend* are all aimed at the older age group. I am sure you will discover a dozen more besides; there's a big market out there, including many regional magazines. Indeed, where once a county might have just one magazine, now they often have three or more.

You may also often read an article in a magazine and think 'So what? I could write that.' I used to do this all the time and it was, in fact, my excuse for not writing anything. So, if you ever see an article and think 'I could have written that', then ask yourself 'why didn't I?' and knuckle down to write some equivalent piece.

Before sending anything to a magazine, you need to study at least three editions. This is to get the flavour of it. Some have a cosy, chatty style; others are deliberately abrasive and interested in abseiling grannies rather than knitting patterns. Look at the adverts, read the letters page, immerse yourself in the feel of the magazine. Do you have a piece that would fit? Check out the details of the magazine in one of the annual writer's guides (See Handbooks in Appendix B). Get on their website and see if they take freelance contributions and have guidelines for contributors. Some don't; others may be entirely freelance-written. Don't forget that many professional associations have their own in-house magazines that may offer you a home for an article if it's relevant.

You will need to tailor any piece you write to its potential home. If a magazine has a slot for nostalgia articles of 800 words, it's pointless sending them one of 2,000. If a magazine never prints poems, there is no point in writing 'I know you never normally print poems, but I'm sure that this one about the death of my cat Tiddles when I was only seven years old will touch a nerve with many of your readers.'

Once you have found a likely target for your work and adjusted your piece to suit that magazine, you need to present your work professionally to the editor. Once again, the magazine's website will probably carry details of how to do this. If not, then you should make sure that the article itself is double-spaced, that you have good wide margins, numbered pages and somewhere you have included your name, address, phone number and email. Somewhere at the foot of the page, it is reasonable to include your name alongside the copyright symbol. However, don't splatter the copyright symbol all over the place. It is the sign of the over-anxious amateur, terrified lest the wicked editor is going to rip off his wonderful idea. Frankly, my experience has shown that the more anxious someone has been about their idea being stolen, the poorer that idea is. Editors have probably had the same experience. They're inundated with material and are looking for reasons not to publish your work.

I still occasionally send my work by post, just because I think it's too easy for an editor to simply press the delete button on anything emailed. However, the usual rules apply for emails and letters - keep it short, to the point, be polite ... you know the sort of thing.

Don't use a pen-name unless you are writing about something that is hugely personal and you need to keep your identity a secret. Pen-names are for amateurs and the kinds of prolific novelists who write in different genres and so have different readerships.

If you haven't had a reply from the magazine within 6-8 weeks, it is reasonable to follow up with a query email. It's probably best to avoid phoning editors. They don't like interruptions and may feel as though you are hassling them. If you get no reply, then re-work the piece and send it to the next magazine on your hit list.

Writing for magazines can be very rewarding. Whilst you are unlikely to make a personal fortune from it, some magazines do pay quite handsomely for well-written pieces that their readers will enjoy. There is no reason why you couldn't use extracts from your life story as a springboard for developing a part-time career writing about all sorts of different issues for magazines.

Publishing Your Life Story

You may, however, feel that rather than trying to sell extracts – or indeed as well as selling extracts – from your work, you would like to see your finished work in some kind of permanent form.

This could range from simple home-publishing, to attempting to sell your book to a publisher. Let's look at some of these options.

Home Publishing

For most of you reading this book, home publishing will be what you are aiming to do. You will be recording parts of your life for your children and grandchildren, so that they know what your experiences were.

You can make your home published book as inexpensive or as dear as you want. The cheapest way to produce a 'book' is to print on A4 pages, then use a hole punch and a ribbon to tie the whole together. If you scan in photographs, you can have illustrations as well.

A step up from this is to use some kind of plastic binding. Most copy shops and a large number of libraries have the facilities to put some kind of plastic binder on your finished work. In fact, binding machines are now so cheap, that you could probably share the cost of one round a writers' group (if you belong to one), or pick one up second-hand and re-sell it when you've finished. I use one of these basic plastic spine binders to make up any booklets I use when I'm teaching. They're a bit fiddly to use to begin with, but once you get the knack, it's an easy way of making a fistful of pages look a tad smarter than a treasury tag. It's also easier to read than if you put it into a ring-binder.

If you're looking for something a little grander, there are specialist binders in almost every university town who put together dissertations and doctoral theses. If you're only producing a handful of presentation copies, this might be worth the added expense. In fact, what could be a greater personalised present than giving your family a handsomely-bound copy of your life story?

Submitting Your Work to an Agent or Publisher

Some of you may be more ambitious. You might think that your story deserves a wider audience. It may well do, but if you're going down the route of trying to find an agent or a publisher, you have to be prepared to be disappointed. If selling articles is hard, then selling a full-scale book is even harder. The story of your life may make fascinating reading for your family, but that does not mean that it will make fascinating reading for the wider public.

Publishing is a commercial business. Publishers need to make a profit in order to survive. Agents and publishers are inundated with material. For every *Angela's Ashes* they see, they have to sift through a thousand or more stories that range from the inept and the banal to the near-misses. Yes, we all know the tales of the masterpiece that was rejected by seventy-five publishers. Unfortunately, whilst there may be a rare exception, books that are rejected repeatedly with nothing more than a standard rejection letter are normally rejected for good reasons.

Of course, if you've followed the advice in this book, I'd like to think you stand a better chance than most. So, if you can withstand the battering that trying to sell your work to publishers can inflict on your ego, then here's what you have to do.

First of all, there's a bit of a Catch 22 in publishing. It's difficult to get a book published without an agent and difficult to get an agent without a book deal in place. If this is the only book you intend writing, then you probably don't need an agent. To begin with, stick to finding a publisher. You can always interest an agent at a later stage if you are suddenly offered a world-beating deal.

Make a list of publishers who might be interested in your work. Get down to your library and local bookshop, surf the web and identify which publishers produce books like yours. You can also find out more about which publishers to approach using one of the annual guides for writers (see Appendix B). Some will only be interested in approaches from agents. Forget them for the time being and concentrate on those who will accept unsolicited manuscripts.

Most of those publishers who can be approached without an agent ask for a sample of your writing and a synopsis. Publishers (or agents for that matter) do not want to see an entire manuscript at first. They want to know that you can write and that you have a good story to tell. They can probably do that from one page of your writing. In fact, one of the largest agencies in the country asks children's authors to submit just one paragraph from their book, along with a synopsis. That's how tough it can be.

As a general guide, send two or three chapters at most, along with a short covering letter and a brief synopsis of your book. Your synopsis should tell the reader about the main characters and events in the book. It should also be interesting. Writing a synopsis is hard work. It is your calling card. Spend time working it up into an interesting little read in its own right. Would the synopsis tempt you to read the book?

You then need to write a covering letter. This should be kept simple, stating the title of the book and any relevant information. Don't try to be clever, funny or over-elaborate. What you are sending is a business proposal. It needs to be crisp and to the point. Then, having established whether your targets want electronic or postal submissions, send your chapters and synopsis, together with a covering letter (or whatever it is they specifically ask for) to the first half-dozen publishers on your list.

Publishers don't particularly like this. They like to think they're the only ones getting a chance to see your submission, but sometimes a publisher will sit on a manuscript for as long as six months. Frankly, you can't wait that long for an outcome. When I tell my students this, they always worry about what might happen if two publishers are interested in the same book. Frankly, this sounds like an ideal world. If you're selling your house and you've got two potential buyers, it's bound to push up the price. Having two publishers interested looks to me like a problem worth trying to handle.

Make sure you keep a good record of where you have sent your work. As each rejection comes in (and they will), then send your pack to the next publisher on your list, so that you've always got six or so publishers on the go. Now be prepared to suffer rejection; all writers are rejected at some point or other. You have to be prepared for it. Rejection is hard to take. One of the difficulties with rejection is that it is rare for either magazine editors or publishers to give a reason for it. Quite simply, it's not their job. Nor is it their job to explain to us what we could do to a piece to make it of publishable standard. If they did that, then they wouldn't have time to do any publishing or editing.

Most letters are standard rejection letters. They are normally polite, but restrained and use phrases such as 'not suitable' or 'unlikely to fit with our existing portfolio' and explain how many zillions of submissions they have each day. Occasionally, an editor or publisher will come back with something a little more personal. 'I really liked the tone of this, but we did a similar piece in Issue 66' is an indication that you have a potentially saleable item on your hands. See these kinds of rejections in as positive a light as you can. They are genuine near-misses. Next time, you might be luckier.

Self-publishing

If you find that you are rejected by every publisher around, then you might think of publishing the book yourself. By this, I mean that you might want to produce what you have written as something more than a bound manuscript. You want your book to look just like the ones that appear on the shelves in the shops.

Self-publishing has a long and illustrious history. Beatrix Potter published the first edition of *Peter Rabbit* using her own money. Virginia Wolf published several of her works herself. However, these were wealthy, upper middle-class ladies, who could afford to self-publish and lose a few bob without having to worry about the mortgage.

In the past decade, self-publishing has altered incredibly. Once it was a hugely expensive business, whereby you had to order at least several hundred copies. Self-publishers ended up with garages full of boxes of books and angry letters from the bank manager. Now, with print-on-demand, short-run printing and various e-book formats, it's comparatively cheap. If this path interests you, then an evening on the web should give you plenty of information to get started.

However, if you're thinking of producing a less-ambitious volume, say of 32 to 64 pages, then publishing in A5 format is a possibility. Approach local printers for a price. Whatever they tell you it will cost per unit, you then need to put a cover price of around four times that amount to ensure that you cover all your costs and allow for discounts to shops, etc. You will find that the unit cost of each book will be cheaper the more you have printed. Be realistic. If you think you can sell 200 copies, have 200 copies printed. You can always have extras made. It may make the unit cost more expensive, but it is preferable to having 1,000 booklets sitting rotting in the garden shed. I've done this a few times for copies of anthologies of various projects I've been involved with. Books are harder to sell than you think.

Vanity Publishing

If you decide to self-publish a book, you are in charge of its production. There are companies who will take over the process for you and provide you with however many copies you want. These companies are entirely respectable printing businesses who take on the extra duties of obtaining an ISBN number and bar-code (vital to bookshops) typesetting, design and so on.

However, there are some sharks in these waters. They are often referred to as 'vanity publishers', because, quite simply, they play on our vanity. They tell us that our manuscript is 'remarkable', 'refreshing', 'the best thing I have read in years'. They dangle likely sales figures that are way in excess of anything you're honestly, likely to achieve. Then they sting you for a 'contribution to printing costs'.

The autobiographer is easy prey for a vanity publisher. We all think our story should be read by the widest possible audience. When it is turned down by the umpteenth publisher, you look to those you'll have to pay yourself to publish. You have put so much of yourself – your time, let's face it, your life – into this book, that it is going to see the light of day no matter what. The excellent Jonathon Clifford has been running a campaign for many years to put an end to the worst excesses of vanity publishing.

On his website, he quotes the British Standards Authority, who describe vanity publishers as 'any company which charges a client to publish a book; or offers to include short stories, poems or other literary or artistic material in an anthology and then invites those included to buy a copy of that anthology.'

The trouble with vanity presses is that they can easily suck you in. I know of one elderly gentleman, who lost over a thousand pounds when a 'subsidy publisher' (another name by which they lurk) went bust. Tantalizingly, his book had been printed, but due to the legal wrangling over the assets of the company, they were stuck in a warehouse. It was a book of incredibly badly-written poetry that was essentially unpublishable, but that didn't stop them talking him up.

There are also horror stories of people parting with even more money than this to find that, yes, they do have 2,000 copies of their book, but the essential clause that said the pages of their book would be bound together was missing from the contract. What they've really got is 350,000 sheets of paper.

Mainstream publishers are generally realistic when it comes to selling your book. OK, occasionally they shell out ludicrous sums for works by well-known TV stars, politicians and footballers, but in the main they can tell how many copies a book will sell. Vanity publishers will heap praise on even the direst of drivel - there's no limit to the number of copies of your book they will sell. And make sure you've got the right visas in your passport, because the world book tour beckons.

Be very careful. There's a thin line between vanity publishers and people who will genuinely help you self-publish your book. If you're thinking of self-publishing using a company, then ask them to put you in touch with other customers. And double-check that these really are customers.

Final Word

Selling anything autobiographical to magazines, agents or publishers is hard work. There are thousands of people just like yourself out there, who have important stories to tell. Don't be dismayed if you find that no-one wants to publish your work for commercial gain. Simply produce a smart home-made version of your work, written to the highest possible standards you can achieve, and your family will be left with an amazing record of your life.

****

Appendix A – Further Reading
Autobiographies, Memoirs, Life Stories

These are some autobiographies I have enjoyed over the years that I think are worth looking at. I've tried to include a range of tastes, so hopefully there'll be something of use to you here. I've tried to include humour as well as downright misery and shades in between.

Reading is such a personal experience that what one person finds compelling can drive another mad. You also probably want to read about the people you want to read about. If you're into motor racing, then you'll want to read autobiographies of famous drivers. If you like films, then those of actors and directors. Don't forget that many of these books have been ghost-written and sometimes are appallingly shoddy - *I passed the ball to Smithy and ran into the box. He knocked it over to me. I headed it and it went in. Three-nil. Job done.*

There's no order to what now follows, so feel free to pick and choose at random, or even better, make some choices of your own.

Boy - Tales of Childhood by Roald Dahl, first published in 1984

Roald Dahl has such an easy style, he makes writing look simple. Although the book does sometimes feel like a diatribe against corporal punishment, the way Dahl captures the time and social milieu of his boyhood is excellent. Even if you don't like the book, the preface is worth using as a handy guide for your own writing. There's also follow-up called *Going Solo*, from 1986, which deals with Dahl's years in Africa and his exploits in the Second World

War. With Dahl's pithy, readable writing style, you can easily manage both short books in an afternoon.

If This is a Man by Primo Levi, first published in Italian in 1958

Levi survived Hitler's death camps. Rarely can there have been anything on earth as hideously de-humanising as Nazi concentration camps, but Levi's writing is not self-pitying. He tells his story directly. The compassion arises from the situations he describes and not from the overwrought use of sentimental language. Levi eventually committed suicide - it's possible that he felt bad for surviving the camps when so many died - and knowing this as you read makes his words even more compelling. My copy is a double edition with Levi's *The Truce*, which tells of how he walked all the way back from Auschwitz to Turin (more-or-less via Minsk).

Cider with Rosie by Laurie Lee, first published in 1959

Laurie Lee was a poet, but his series of autobiographical books are what brought him fame. *Cider with Rosie* is the best of the series. I think it would be hard to emulate his poet's choice of words, but I love the way the book manages to progress chronologically, as well as being divided into themed chapters. In some ways the book is very simple - there are very few moments of genuine high drama, but it is beautifully told and conjures up a village world that's now gone. That said, his writing is perhaps a little rich for the modern palate - he is highly descriptive. If you love clever description, I suspect you'll adore it. If you want something fast-paced, you may end up gnawing the leg off the table.

Portrait of the Artist as a Young Man by James Joyce, first published in instalments 1914-1915

I actually studied this book at school, which should have put me off for life. It's not everyone's cup of tea, but it's interesting the way the language of the book develops as the child becomes older. It's hard to work out how much is novelised and how much genuine autobiography. What is for sure is that it is written extremely cleverly. The book starts with the baby language of a tot in the nursery and changes as Joyce gets older. It's also a piece of stream-of-consciousness writing, so if you like your writing a tad plainer it may not be for you. At least try the first 30 or 40 pages. Joyce actually threw an early version on the fire himself. You might be tempted to as well.

The Moon's A Balloon by David Niven, first published in 1972

Often, celebrity autobiographies are a dismal hotchpotch of name-droppings. Niven's book is full of the names of Hollywood Greats, but also rammed with stories of Hollywood's Golden Age. He manages to make it all sound like one great big adventure. I don't know how much of it is true, but I don't really care. These are highly-polished anecdotes that are often hilariously funny. They also date from a time when celebrity gossip was a much more surface, less invasive affair than it is now, so they felt very revelatory at the time.

Fever Pitch by Nick Hornby, first published in 1992

I'm not sure if you have to like football to like this book. It's worth getting from the library at the very least to see how he moves from one topic to the next even if you aren't keen on the game, because what is interesting is the way in which Hornby, with wonderful self-irony, examines his obsession with Arsenal football club and relates it to other aspects of existence. He pegs what's happening in his personal life - especially his love life - around various games at Highbury Stadium. It's also very funny.

Adolf Hitler – My Part in His Downfall by Spike Milligan, first published in 1971

If you don't like Spike Milligan, you'll hate this book. I happen to think he was one of the funniest men who ever lived. He wrote of his call-up papers that he received an envelope and inside 'there was a cunningly disguised invitation to partake in World War II'. Milligan writes 'all the salient facts are true', but he also includes ridiculous obviously made-up material, such as fake telegrams from high-ranking German officials. He also peppers it with diary entries and contemporary photographs. It's a great antidote to all those 'how I won the war single-handedly' books that used to appear every other year, normally written by someone who was in the Catering Corps and never got further than Chatham.

Post Office by Charles Bukowski, first published in 1971

As with Milligan, if you don't tune into Bukowski's humour, you won't think much of this autobiographical novel. However, even if you don't like Bukowski's drinking, womanising and gambling (hey, a guy should have hobbies), then you might like the idea that he simply takes a cross-section of his life – his years working for the U.S. Post Office – and writes about that. His publisher offered Bukowski $100 a week if he left his job at the post office and wrote full time. Bukowski delivered the manuscript of this book three weeks later. All of Bukowski's novels are based on his own drink-sodden life, and if you're easily offended, you simply won't like him.

Oranges are not the Only Fruit by Jeanette Winterson, first published in 1985

I'm not too keen on the little allegorical sections of the book, but Winterson's tales of her religious upbringing are witty, humorous and ultimately, sad. It's a novelized version of her early years and she has since published her memoirs as *Why Be Happy When You Could Be Normal.* Winterson's writings on her mother's lack of understanding of her lesbianism are excellent and the title of the actual memoir comes from a juicy one-liner from her adoptive mother. Certainly worth trying out both books to see which one wins out for you.

Three Men in a Boat by Jerome K Jerome, first published in 1889

Although well over 100 years old, this is a comedy classic of exaggerated memoir. Jerome essentially invented the comedy travelogue. Jerome, two of his friends and a dog hire a covered rowing-boat for a holiday on the Thames. Of course it has dated, but there are still elements of it that are laugh-out-loud funny to this day. Some of the set-piece comedy routines are great - who can resist the episode where, unable to find the correct train at Waterloo Station, they bribe the train-driver to take them to Kingston or the fishermen's tales of catching a huge trout, now stuffed in a glass case? There are also one-liners that stand the test of time, although admittedly some references have dated really badly. He followed it up with *Three Men on the Bummel,* which is intermittently funny.

The Kiss by Kathryn Harrison, first published in 1997

A bizarre subject – the author's incestuous affair with her estranged father. Yes, I know. It's extraordinarily confessional. She's also at least partly guilty. This is no raping of a pre-pubescent child; she is 20 when the incest starts and old enough to know what she's doing. Several critics thought she'd have been better off keeping quiet about it or at least only sharing it with her psychologist. Some also found her prose rather annoying - a sort of sub-Sylvia Plath. It's not my normal diet, I confess, but I thought it was beautifully written and, yes, also toe-curling in parts. If you're going to read hugely confessional writing, then at least Harrison tries to give hers a bit of style.

In the Blood by Andrew Motion, first published in 2006

Another memoir of childhood. Motion's mother had a terrible hunting accident when he was 16. When he sees her in his hospital bed, he vows to try to keep all the details of his life up until this point. There's an awful lot of how awful boys' boarding schools were in here as there is in Roald Dahl's *Boy*. And perhaps not a lot happens, but it happens in rich prose. Andrew Motion was the UK's Poet Laureate for a time and he has a poet's sensibility for detail.

Goodbye to All That by Robert Graves, first published in 1929

We know from the famous war poets, such as Wilfred Owen and Siegfried Sassoon how dreadful the Great War was. Graves, like Owen and Sassoon was a young officer in the trenches. He covers not only the war years, but also that golden age pre-war when those with money could enjoy a fabulously comfortable lifestyle. Of course, this makes life on the Western Front even more shocking, where bungling and the resultant carnage left their mark on him both mentally and physically.

Testament of Youth by Vera Brittain, first published in 1933

Those back home were also affected dramatically by the events of the Great War. Brittain's brother and her fiancé were both killed in Flanders. Brittain herself served as a nurse, including spending time in France. The first volume deals not only with this, but is also an account of the way in which women were jostling for a position in British society. Eventually, with an Oxbridge degree in place, she becomes a journalist. There's a hugely fierce intelligence at work here and it also serves to remind us of the way in which women have been afforded fewer opportunities than men.

I Know Why the Caged Bird Sings by Maya Angelou, first published in 1969

Maya Angelou went on to publish another six books of autobiography, but if she'd only written this one, you'd know you're in the presence of greatness. The caged bird of the title is another way of referring to slaves. This is the story of a young, black girl in a society that isn't kind to girls and if they have the wrong colour skin, life is even tougher. And if you live in the southern states of the USA … It's not only worth reading for content, but the way in which Angelou writes about her life in little episodes could be a useful template for you.

My Family and Other Animals by Gerald Durrell, first published in 1956

It's perhaps a little dated now, but Durrell's tales of family life on Corfu has a cracking cast of eccentrics – and not just the Durrell family. They keep on televising this and/or versions of the Durrells' story, which is a pity. Like *Cider with Rosie*, there's not enough story to keep the momentum of a TV programme going, so you end up with Sunday evening pretty pictures of a sun-drenched Corfu and caricatures of the family. The book is also interesting if you're especially keen on natural history.

On the Road by Jack Kerouac, first published in 1957

This is another novelised memoir in which the real people in Kerouac's life appear in the thinnest of disguises in his fast-paced road trip of a book. It captures a time post-war when the beat generation were testing out new freedoms and jazz, marijuana and the first hints of sexual liberation were coming into fashion. Famously, Kerouac typed the draft manuscript on a continuous roll of paper and is also supposed to have written it in a Benzedrine-driven three-week fury. It's not without its faults, but it still pulses. It's best read in your late teens. Not a teenager? Try it anyway.

The Belljar by Sylvia Plath, first published in 1963

Sylvia Plath is probably most famous for being the suicidal wife of Ted Hughes. She was a great poet in her own right and this is an autobiographical novel about her early adulthood that goes some way to explaining just how fragile a person she was. It charts a descent into depression in a way that seems all too eerie when you look at Plath's own life. This too is best read when you're in your late teens. Plath, like Hughes, was a poet and her collection *Ariel* is also extremely autobiographical. If you enjoy those poems, then you should also try Hughes's *Birthday Letters*, a collection of poems written over a period of more than 20 years following her death, addressed to Plath.

Wild Swans: Three Daughters of China by Jung Chang, first published in 1991

Chang traces the stories of her grandmother, her mother and herself in China. We move from her grandmother's bound feet (they were supposed to make you walk more daintily), via the story of her mother's rise in the communist party to her parents' fall from grace and to Chang's 're-education' amongst Chinese peasants. Just be glad you didn't live in communist China.

Stasiland by Anna Funder, first published in 2003

… or for that matter in communist East Germany before the wall came tumbling down. By 1989, the year the wall fell, one in every fifty East Germans was an informer to the dreaded secret police, the Stasi. Funder goes on a journey to track down both spies and spied upon, so although it's not quite an autobiography, we do learn about the author through her tales of saints and sinners and by her reflections on what took place.

The Diving Bell and the Butterfly by Jean-Dominique Bauby, originally published in French in 1997

Bauby was a magazine editor who suffered a stroke, was left in a coma for three weeks, then when he awoke he had what is called locked-in syndrome. He was virtually paralysed, but knew what was happening around him. The whole book was dictated by blinking. A secretary would read out the letters of the alphabet in frequency order (E being the most common letter in French) and Bauby would wink his remaining good eye to indicate which letter the secretary needed to write down at a rate of two minutes per word.

The Year of Magical Thinking by Joan Didion, first published in 2005

Joan Didion's daughter was already dangerously ill in hospital when Didion's husband died of a heart attack. This book is the story of how Didion copes with her grief, the magical thinking being the belief that if she did things a certain way, her husband would come back. Didion already had a big reputation for real-life essays when this book came out. She followed it up with another meditation on death, *Blue Nights*, when her daughter also died.

A Heartbreaking Work of Staggering Genius by Dave Eggers, first published in 2000

Eggers won't be everyone's cup of tea, but his prose is vibrant. This is the story of how as a 20-something, Eggers suddenly finds himself responsible for his much younger brother, following the death of his parents. Eggers is a founder and editor of the literary magazine McSweeney's, which is held in high regard by the literati.

Portrait of the Artist as a Young Dog by Dylan Thomas, first published in 1940

If you like your prose poetic and ambitious and enjoy touches of irreverence and comedy, then Dylan Thomas's evocation of episodes in his early life is well worth the read. It's also interesting to see the way in which episodic writing can sometimes work much more powerfully than a chronological narrative. You'll also enjoy *A Child's Christmas in Wales.*

Angela's Ashes by Frank McCourt, first published in 1996

McCourt may not have invented the misery memoir (that was probably Thomas De Quincey's *Confessions of an English Opium-eater*, way back in 1821), but this book set off a bit of a trend. Of the imitators that followed, few were as well written. McCourt's childhood is one of slum-dwelling poverty with an alcoholic father who squanders what little he earns. Of course, McCourt eventually triumphs over all this - that's in the nature of misery memoirs. If you want your books to have barrel-loads of laughs, this isn't for you.

Me Talk Pretty One Day by David Sedaris, first published in 2000

As an antidote to a misery memoir, then why not spend an evening in the company of David Sedaris. You may have heard him on the radio reading out his stories of real life. He's very funny and this book is just a series of reflections and anecdotes about his life - personal essays if you will. We may not be as funny as him, but the actual method of simply re-telling stories as they occur to you might be one way of writing your story that you could consider.

The Book of Life - A Compendium of the Best Autobiographical and Memoir Writing, edited by Eve Claxton

I came across this book the best way you can find one - accidentally- and bought a used copy for a handful of coins. It is one the best buys I've ever made. Indeed, I've used it as a resource throughout this book. It's a heavy beast, but is full of snippets organized by the themes of Beginnings, Youth, Middle and Towards the End. There is something in here for everyone and because there are so many styles and topics covered, then if you're not interested by one extract, you can simply move onto the next.

****

Appendix B – Useful Reference Books

Everyone has their own preferred reference books. Despite the rise of the Internet, I still have a shelf of this kind of thing. Perhaps gone are the days when you need a decent encyclopaedia as there's so much available on-line. However, it is worth having the following:

Everyday Reference

A decent dictionary - I use Penguin's *The New English Dictionary*. It's worth getting a recent one as so many new, technological/technical words enter the language all the time.

A good quality thesaurus - *Roget's Thesaurus* or *The Oxford Paperback Thesaurus* are the two that I tend to prefer. Most word-processing programs have a built-in thesaurus, but they are rarely comprehensive enough. *The Oxford Dictionary of Synonyms and Antonyms* is also a useful guide.

Historical Sourcebooks

Chronology of the 20th Century . There are several of these available, many are more directed towards events in the USA.

Robert Opie Scrapbooks. There are several of these, covering different decades, the war years, etc. They are crammed with pictures of memorabilia and are a fabulous resource for reminding you of packaging, trends, usic and television. They are expensive, but you could always get them from your local library. Old-style.

Grammar, Punctuation, Style etc.

If you feel insecure about your English and want a bit of guidance, I might as well give my own book *Writing Good, Plain English* a bit of a plug (again). It imagines that the would-be writer has a longish project to write and helps people through the process. One company in Australia has even bought 600 copies for its staff (if that's any recommendation). It's with the same publisher as this book.

Penguin Guide to Punctuation - plenty of useful examples. I'm always having to look up how to punctuate dialogue, even now.

Oxford Style Manual - if you really want to get technical, this one covers everything from proofreaders marks to punctuation to how to present indexes, quotations and references. Not a book for the faint-hearted.

Handbooks for Writers

If you want to start selling your work, then you will find one of these two books essential reading. There's not much to choose between them. Both are published annually. I buy them alternate years:

The Writer's Handbook, edited by Barry Turner, published by Macmillan

Writers and Artists Yearbook, published by A & C Black

Books on Writing

If you get the writing bug and want to take your writing further, you might find you want to delve into other areas of writing. There are many books available on the subject.

As writing books are so individual, it is probably worth testing them out at the library if you can before buying the ones you like best and will continue to refer to. I would recommend the following general books:

How to Write a Damn Good Novel by James N. Frey (not the James Frey who embroidered his life story)

Writing Fiction: A Guide to Narrative Craft by Janet Burroway and Elizabeth Stuckey-French

On Writing by Stephen King

The Creative Writing Coursebook by Julia Bell and Paul Magrs,

The Creative Writing Workbook by John Singleton

Becoming a Writer by Dorothea Brande

****